DEEP STALL

Deep Stall

The Turbulent Story of Boeing Commercial Airplanes

PHILIP K. LAWRENCE
University of the West of England, UK
and
DAVID W. THORNTON
Campbell University, USA

ASHGATE

Published by
Ashgate Publishing Limited
Gower House
Croft Road
Aldershot
Hampshire GU11 3HR
England

Ashgate Publishing Company
Suite 420
101 Cherry Street
Burlington, VT 05401-4405
USA

Ashgate website: http://www.ashgate.com

British Library Cataloguing in Publication Data
Lawrence, Philip K.
  Deep stall : the turbulent story of Boeing Commercial
  Airplanes
  1.Boeing Aerospace Company 2.Boeing Commercial Airplane
  Company 3.Aircraft industry - United States - History
  4.Boeing airplanes - History
  I.Title II.Thornton, David Weldon, 1957-
  338.4'762913334'0973

Library of Congress Cataloging-in-Publication Data
Lawrence, Philip K.
  Deep stall : the turbulent story of Boeing commercial airplanes / by Philip K.
Lawrence and David W. Thornton.
        p. cm.
  Includes bibliographical references and index.
  ISBN 0-7546-4626-2
  1. Boeing airplanes--History. 2. Boeing Aircraft Company--History. I. Thornton,
David Weldon, 1957- II. Title

  TL686.B65L39 2005
  629.133'349'0973--dc22

                                                              2005015266

ISBN-10: 0 7546 4626 2

Printed in Great Britain by MPG Books Ltd, Bodmin, Cornwall

Contents

List of Figures

List of Tables

Acknowledgements

Writing a book is often a collective endeavour. We wish to express our thanks to a number of a number of individuals who have given us valuable support on this project. Group Captain (Rtd) Jeff Turner assisted with technical aspects of the analysis and provided original research material for the authors. Our house designer, Charles Stocks of Storm Creative, gave sterling help with graphics and pictures. Guy Loft, our editor at Ashgate, was a great enthusiast for the book and also an efficient and effective collaborator. Benita Lawrence read the manuscript and identified gaps and inconsistencies. A number of Boeing employees supplied key insights, but have asked to remain anonymous. Our greatest debt is to Sean Rothman, who as well as giving technical advice about the Boeing 757 and the 767, did the overall editing and production task. Bottles of Chateau Dassault and the music of Pink Floyd also sustained us through some of the more difficult moments.

List of Abbreviations

AAF	Army Air Force
AI	Airbus Industrie
AIA	Aerospace Industries Association
AST	Advanced Subsonic Technology program
AWACS	Airborne Warning And Control System
BAC	British Aircraft Corporation
BAe	British Aerospace
BCA	Boeing Commercial Airplanes
BOAC	British Overseas Airways Corporation
CAC	Commercial Airplanes Company
CEO	Chief Executive Officer
COTA	Congressional Office of Technology Assessment
CRT	Cathode Ray Tube
CTDC	Civil Transport Development Corporation
DCAC	Define and Control Aircraft Configuration
DISCS	Domestic International Sales Corporations
DM	Deutschmarks
DOC	Direct Operating Costs
DoD	Department of Defense
EADS	European Aeronautics Defence & Space Company
EEC	European Economic Community
ETOPS	Extended-range Twin Engine Operations
EU	European Union
FAA	Federal Aviation Agency (1958-1967)
FAA	Federal Aviation Administration (April 1967 onwards)
FBW	Fly-by-wire
FFCC	Forward-Facing Crew Cockpit
FMCS	Flight Management Computer System
FMS	Flight Management System
FOREX	Foreign Exchange
FSCS	Foreign Sales Corporations
GATT	General Agreement on Tariffs and Trade
GE	General Electric
GIE	*Groupement d'Interet Economique*
HSA	Hawker Siddeley Aviation
HSR	High Speed Research Program
IBM	International Business Machines
ICC	Interstate Commerce Commission

JAL	Japan Airlines
JSF	Joint Strike Fighter
LCA	Large Commercial Aircraft
MBA	Master of Business Administration
MBB	Messerschmitt Bölkow-Blohm
MDC	McDonnell Douglas Corporation
MIT	Massachusetts Institute of Technology
METI	Ministry of Economy, Trade & Industry
MITI	Ministry for International Trade & Industry
MRM	Manufacturing Resource Management
NACA	National Advisory Committee for Aeronautics
NAMC	Nihon Aircraft Manufacturing Company
NASA	National Aeronautics & Space Administration
NG	Next-Generation
PAC	President's Advisory Committee on Supersonic Transport
P&W	Pratt & Whitney
OPEC	Organization of Petroleum Exporting Countries
R&D	Research & Development
R&T	Research & Technology
SARS	Severe Acute Respiratory Syndrome
SST	Supersonic Transport
STOVL	Short Take Off & Vertical Landing
TWA	Transcontinental & Western Air (1929-1945)
TWA	Trans World Airlines (1945 onwards)
UK	United Kingdom
US	United States
USA	United States of America
USAF	United States Air Force
USSR	Union of Soviet Socialist Republics
USTR	United States Trade Representative
WTO	World Trade Organization

Preface

For 35 years the Boeing company dominated the world of civil jet transport manufacture. But in the early 21st century that dominance has evaporated and the number one position now belongs to the European company, Airbus. By any standards this is an extraordinary transformation. When Airbus began life in 1970 few would have countenanced the possibility of its rise to world leadership. Even more remarkably, this achievement has happened in a period when the US economy has outperformed its European competitors and there is much gloom in evidence regarding European economic prospects. The financial press are full of stories praising the neo-liberal Anglo-Saxon economic model of the US.

This book assesses the reasons for Boeing's decline. The decline of the US company is remarkable. In an oligopolistic industry, where barriers to entry are high, large incumbent firms have an enormous advantage over new entrants. The existing scale economies and the learning curve experience should make the incumbent firm almost invulnerable, because of the vast sunk costs facing the new comer and the much higher manufacturing costs at the top of the learning curve. But this assumes a continuing strategic drive for market leadership and a focus on dominance, not just profit.

As we outline below, in previous decades Boeing had exactly this strategic orientation. But more recently, as the analysis shows, the US company has made key errors and underestimated the significance of *strategic value*; we define this term as investment in new technology and product development in order to leverage future market success. As we indicate below, after the daring decision to build the 747, Boeing pursued an extremely conservative product strategy of producing derivative aircraft in order to avoid the cost of developing new models. Such a policy delivered a short-term gain in terms of cash flow and appeased shareholders, but in our view ultimately represented a strategy of inevitable failure.

This failure also impacts on the national strategic value of Boeing to the United States. National strategic value concerns the contribution made to the US economy in terms of jobs, technology, Intellectual Property Rights, exports and overall capability. From this perspective a company engaged in a strategic industry can be seen as a national asset. However, we believe that in recent years Boeing has declined in significance as a US national asset. A key symptom of this process is the exporting of US jobs and technology via offset agreements and alliances with partners in Asia. In effect, US capability is being exported overseas.

Boeing's fall from market leadership also represents an extraordinary failure in US public policy for the aerospace industry. Contrary to the nostrums of neo-liberal economics about *laissez-faire*, the US company has benefited from much government support, (Lawrence, 2001, pp. 46-85). In the early years this was via the largesse provided by government air mail contracts. However, over the long haul Boeing has been sustained at critical periods by military sales and has also successfully utilized technologies in commercial products developed and paid for by the US government, either via NASA or the Department of Defense (DoD). As Laura Tyson notes such support from government represents 'a makeshift, but nonetheless effective industrial policy', (Tyson, 1992, p. 157). On the wider canvas of macro-economic management the European approach to the aeronautics industry is no more interventionist than the American fusion of Anglo-Saxon liberalism with military Keynesianism. However, for this sector the European approach of public/private partnership appears to be more successful.

Introduction

Aeronautics as a Strategic Industry

Liberal economists struggle with strategic industries like aviation and aeronautics. This is because both the supply and demand functions for these industries are influenced by non-market factors. Liberal welfare economists have even argued that sectors such as aerospace ought to be abandoned if they cannot be sustained by the free market. But this is a pure flight of fancy. Contrary to the ideals of liberal economists, the history and success of both aviation and aerospace is significantly entwined with that of the state. The industry is simply too important to have been left to the vicissitudes of the free market and would hardly have existed without state involvement.

Aeronautics is a strategic industry. This is because of its significance for national defense, its creation of high value-added jobs, and its ability to drive forward advanced technology. It is also strategic because it embodies industrial and manufacturing power in advanced engineering. It is a sector strongly associated with national prestige and international status. The large primes in the sector are therefore national strategic assets, operating close to or sometimes even inside the boundaries of state power.

The Perspective of Political Economy

This book assesses the strategic decline of Boeing, the world's foremost aeronautics company. In order to describe and analyze the rise and fall in Boeing's fortunes the authors utilize the theories and perspectives of political economy. This is because a company like Boeing operates in both the market and the polity. During its periods of great success Boeing has pursued a strategy which maximized its significance to the US Department of Defense and also provided technologies, developed at government expense that gave leadership in the commercial market.

We adopt the discipline of political economy here because it takes as its point of departure the notion that the realms of governance and commerce must be studied in conjunction, for either to be comprehended as actually practiced. In this view, in order to understand the structure and dynamics of markets for strategic goods and the related priorities and behaviour of governments, one requires an approach that is interdisciplinary in scope and integrative in nature; a method that explicitly and systematically combines information and insights from the disciplines of both political science and economics.

Commercial aeronautics is an industry for which analysis from a political economy perspective is most appropriate and informative. This is true especially at the international level, where the priorities of sovereign states interact intensively with commercial imperatives of global scale to produce a pattern of government policy and market behaviour that defies comprehension from an angle that is either purely political or economic. Of central concern for much of the last 100 years to national governments from a military standpoint, the strategic characteristics of the technology of powered flight have given it industrial, commercial and financial dimensions that make the sector crucial to economic security. An important source of employment, revenue and prestige, governments look to aerospace, in both its military and commercial dimensions, to place and maintain their countries among the world's most powerful.

In the US the significance of Boeing, the leading aeronautics company, can be seen in the fact that it is America's largest industrial exporter and the key company in the only US manufacturing sector which shows a large trade surplus. In addition, Boeing provides the US with key weapon systems and platforms for both air and space and is pivotal to the strategy for homeland security. Some commentators in the West now doubt the significance of aerospace, but those in the developed world who are dubious about this should look to the drive in the Far East to emulate the West's achievements in this field.

Boeing and the Role of the State

It will be argued here that little sense can be made of the way in which commercial aircraft are manufactured, marketed, and operated for air services without knowledge of the economic, industrial, technological and regulatory context created by national governments. As we shall argue below, this nexus between aeronautics and the state is especially strong because of the military significance of airpower. Particularly during the Cold War, Boeing (and the US aerospace industry as a whole) was a critical resource in the project of defending America and containing world communism. As Gregory Hooks notes, ' ... the airforce could not rely on market forces to maintain the world's largest and most technologically advanced aircraft industry. National security had become equated with industrial policy', (Hooks, 1991, p. 235).

From this perspective, therefore, the US aeronautics industry's historical configuration and dynamics made manifest the priorities and capabilities of the national government. Much of the historical account and analysis below is thus devoted to explaining precisely by what means and to what ends the US state shaped the environment in which aeronautics, and Boeing in particular, evolved. But, of course, this is not just a US phenomenon.

The technological and organization capabilities of all today's aeronautics firms, which make them such salient economic and industrial actors, have to an important degree been created and maintained by financial and human resources harnessed and directed by national governments in Asia, Europe, and North and South America. Without the large and sustained infusions of capital into basic research and product development, often but not always for military purposes, the most basic features that make modern aircraft an effective and attractive mode of transport might well not exist. And without the close regulation of air safety practices and the provision of infrastructure by government, demand for air travel would never have reached the levels of profitability that employ millions in the manufacture and operation of aircraft.

The intensive and mutually conditioning involvement of states throughout the entire history of aeronautics has made it into what is arguably the world's most politicized industry. At the apex of the industry stands the Boeing Company, which is why it represents such an important case deserving of comprehensive study from the perspective of political economy.

Civil and Military Aeronautics

In developing these arguments, we will describe and analyze the close and enduring connection between the military and commercial dimensions of aeronautics as embodied in the Boeing Company. This same connection is also amply evident in the character of the technologies and the activities that comprise the material and organizational foundation of the industry as a whole. Throughout the history of aeronautics, a symbiotic relationship existed between governments and those individuals and organizations able to provide for the needs of the state in military aviation. While governments obtained through such a relationship (either by outright ownership or a variety of contractual arrangements) the material and logistical wherewithal for security, the industrial partner gained access to funding and expertise that could be used to develop technologies and skills applicable to commercial purposes. As Laura Tyson observes, 'All of the nation's commercial aircraft producers have been major defense contractors, at least at critical moments in their development. The enormous flow of federal government contracts has provided profits (and even in some cases covered tooling costs) that could be applied to the development of commercial aircraft', (Tyson, 1992, p. 169).

By no means unique in this regard, aeronautics has been distinctive in the extent to which technologies developed for military use found application in the commercial sphere. All of the important constituent elements of large commercial aircraft today; the design and construction of airframes, high-bypass jet propulsion systems, and interactive flight controls are of military origin, and the firms that build and integrate these systems have extensive experience as military contractors. Hence the study will recount the most important military innovations in design, technology and production techniques, which have had a key impact on the development and manufacture of Boeing's large commercial aircraft.

In addition to the technological and financial importance of military contracts to their success in the civilian sphere, both manufacturers and operators of commercial aircraft have long been the privileged subjects of state largesse and protection from competition, and these subsidies and other forms of preferential treatment have rooted economic nationalism deep in the now global market for commercial aircraft and air services. The examination of the subsidy issue below provides clear evidence of the seriousness with which governments take commercial aeronautics. Moreover, the terms of inter-governmental agreements directly affect the structure and dynamics of the industry.

We will also encounter throughout the historical account the interaction of what can be understood as centripetal and centrifugal forces operating as opposing influences in the aeronautics sector. But this nexus is changing. Today, in the post-Cold War era, some of the national state priorities associated with aeronautics are being undercut by globalization. In general terms globalization is intensifying the clash between national and trans-national dynamics in international business.

The interplay of state priorities with the transnational characteristics of a sector undergoing globalization provides a fascinating glimpse of the clash of economic and political forces in the modern world economy. Companies, such as Boeing, which still seek and need national political and financial support, are engaging in a form of trans-national business partnership that actually undercuts their national strength. In the case of Boeing's newest commercial aircraft, the 787, so much of the program is being done overseas that commentators question the company's commitment to the US. This is the essence of the argument of this book, which charts the strategic decline of a company once at the centre of America's national interest.

Outline of the Argument

The early chapters of the book show Boeing's close relationship with the US state. We show that Boeing's senior managers were skilled and intelligent in positioning Boeing at the interface of state and market, in such a way that government contracts and support often mitigated the risk of the company's commercial projects. By the 1960s this clever use of defense and civil opportunities put Boeing at the top of world aeronautics. However, when Europe began to respond to US dominance through the challenge of Airbus Industrie, Boeing underestimated the threat. When the threat was understood, it was often misinterpreted as resulting from unfair forms of government support. In fact, as we show below, Airbus got a foothold in the market in the 1970s by offering new concepts and technology and listening carefully to what the customer wanted. In the 1990s, as the market position of the two companies approached parity, Boeing appeared to become paralyzed over the question of what new projects to invest in. First, the 747X and then the Sonic Cruiser were abandoned. But even more destructively, the solid and mutually beneficial relationship that Boeing had built with the US DoD was poisoned by a series of scandals associated with unethical business practices. As we show none of this bodes well for the Boeing Company. But of course, whether the decline in the civil market we illustrate is terminal remains to be seen. Needless to say, whatever transpires on the commercial side, Boeing will remain a key player in both the US and the global defense and space businesses.

Chapter 1

Pre-History: The Era Before Civil Jet Transport

Introduction

In the lead up to the centenary of the Wright brothers' first successful flight, North Carolina and Ohio engaged in a running dispute over which state had the right to make public claims as being the location most responsible for the genesis of powered flight. The arguments of both have merit, in that the Wright brothers did important work in both Dayton and Kill Devil Hills; the machines were built in their Ohio shop, but assembled and tested on the windy dunes of the Outer Banks. But in reality the geographical net should be spread more widely. Their achievement of 17 December 1903, the first sustained and propelled flight, was the result of theoretical insight and practical skill, in conjunction with a real willingness to risk life and limb, which drew on the insights, successes and failures of countless others on both sides of the Atlantic, (Solberg, 1979, ch.1). To emphasize the European connection it should also be noted that the Wright brothers obtained their first patent from France and opened their first training school in Paris.

Ironically, the success of 1903 was not followed by instant celebrity, and only a few Americans (and even fewer Europeans) knew of or believed in what the Wright brothers had actually accomplished. It was not until 1909, after successful demonstrations of their flying machine for the US War Department, and similar demonstrations in Europe, that the significance of their achievement was appreciated by the public or by governments, (Bilstein, 1994, pp. 1-11). Glen Curtiss was perhaps better known, having made his start in aviation in 1904, after landing a US Army contract to construct an engine for a dirigible. Along with Alexander Graham Bell, in 1907 Curtiss formed the Aerial Experimentation Association and by 1910 was astounding the nation by flying the 'June Bug' 150 miles from Albany to New York City, with only a single stopover at Poughkeepsie, (Solberg, 1979, p. 8).

Aeronautics and the State

With the sudden growth in public enthusiasm for planes and their pilots, air shows and other demonstrations (all dangerous and many fatal for pilots and spectators alike) were the main uses of early aircraft. But both entrepreneurs and governments recognized that other purposes might be served, with short-range passenger services and experimental mail flights beginning at nearly the same time. Predictably, numerous firms designing and manufacturing planes sprung up, and although investors duly took note the predicted big aviation boom failed to materialize. Indeed, despite the early American successes in aviation, many in US government and industry believed that the United States had begun to fall behind in comparison to European aeronautics. A fact-finding mission organized by the Smithsonian Institution was sent to Europe to investigate developments in Europe, headed by Albert F. Zahm of the Massachusetts Institute of Technology. His report, issued in 1914, led directly to the creation in 1915 of the National Advisory Committee for Aeronautics (NACA), whose mission was to conduct basic research on aeronautical topics with both civil and military application, (Bilstein, 1994, p. 31). Thus, only a dozen years after the Wright Brother's first flight, the United States government had begun to take a deep and abiding interest in aeronautics.

In 1909 the Frenchman Louis Bleriot flew across the English Channel, and the age of powered flight had begun in earnest. It should come as no surprise that this elemental feature of aeronautics would emerge originally in the European context, the fount of the very idea and practice of the state and also the starting place of the two World Wars. The title of Anthony Sampson's insightful history of the world airline industry, *Empires of the Sky,* is particularly apt because it captures in so few words the essential nature of the development of the early aeronautics industry. Often depicted as the achievement of individual heroes, such as the Wright brothers, Bleriot, and Lindbergh, human mastery of the air also has been very much a triumph of governments. To an important degree the entire business of making and flying aircraft, most especially its key economic and technological features, is the concrete manifestation of state priorities. Foremost among these priorities has been self-preservation; it is no accident that the most significant advances in powered flight have been made during wars both hot and cold. If necessity is the mother of invention, then modern aeronautics is the offspring of intense interstate rivalry and conflict: 'In every country the soaring ambitions of the aviators and their financiers came up against the controls and military designs of their governments', (Sampson, 1984, p. 24).

With the advent of powered flight at the turn of the century, European governments felt a pressing need to create a set of rules to regulate the new possibility of regular air transit across international boundaries. With French engineers and pilots playing a leading role in the nascent field of aeronautics (the Wright Brothers notwithstanding), it was appropriate that the first international convention on air navigation convene in Paris in 1910, the first intergovernmental meeting of its kind. While accomplishing important definitional and technical tasks relating to transnational air travel, delegates differed sharply on the central issue at hand, *sovereignty;* the right of states to control the airspace above their territory. They adjourned agreeing to disagree on this key issue, showing that aviation could never be divorced from its political implications.

Boeing and the Emergence of US Aviation Policy

Eugene Rodgers notes that William Boeing had his first experience with flight on 4 July 1914, as he and Conrad Westervelt paid for repeated holiday rides over Lake Washington on a barnstormer's aircraft, (1996, p. 24). The two subsequently bought a seaplane and took flying lessons from Glenn Martin to pursue their new hobby. As the First World War spread across Europe and threatened to involve the US, Boeing and Westervelt came to view airplanes and the ability to build them as crucial to the country's security. Leading promoters of aviation in the Pacific Northwest, the two entrepreneurs began work on a plane to be built from the spruce wood, which was so abundant in the region and designated it the B&W. Although Westervelt was called back East for military service, a determined Boeing drew on his personal wealth to form the Pacific Aero Products Company, and the plane's first test flight took place on 16 June 1916: 'He was clearly getting in on the ground floor: In the whole country, only about four hundred aircraft were built in 1916', (Rodgers, p. 29).

Disappointed in finding no civilian customers for the B&Ws, Boeing brought in engineers to modify the design, and in 1917 convinced the Navy of the virtues of his Model C prototype, winning a contract worth $575,000 for 50 trainer aircraft. Reincorporated as the Boeing Airplane Company, 'the good news put the infant company in business for keeps', (Rodgers, p. 31). More navy business followed as Boeing was contracted to build 50 flying boats on license from Curtiss, work that dovetailed nicely with Boeing's shipbuilding experience. But such heavy reliance on military contracts made the company vulnerable to political developments, with both labour and management subject to the vagaries of procurement decisions. As Rodgers puts it: 'November 11 1918, was a great day for the bloodied world but a bad day for Boeing's business: The Great War in Europe ended', (Rodgers, p. 32). The flying boat order was immediately cut in half, and the layoff of half the workforce quickly followed, as the company unsuccessfully sought to diversify into wood products.

At the dawn of the aviation era, the US was less concerned about supporting the nascent industry than its European neighbours. Perhaps unfairly, the US aviation industry had emerged from the First World War publicly discredited and without a clear sense of mission or future direction. Although the NACA (National Advisory Committee for Aeronautics) had been formed in 1915 to undertake research basic to all aspects of aviation and flight, its mission became more militarily oriented as time passed, and its budget remained small. Recognizing the dangers posed by the rapid post-war contraction of military orders, the industry sought to increase public and governmental awareness of the importance of its products, primarily through the Manufacturers Aircraft Association set up during the war to coordinate production. Its chairman, Samuel Stewart Bradley, accompanied a delegation to Great Britain led by Assistant Secretary of War, Benedict Crowell (the Crowell Commission) in the summer of 1919 and came back convinced of the necessity for the United States (like every industrial nation) to maintain a viable capacity in aviation, both civil and military. But the time was not yet ripe for an active US government role in aviation. As Nick Komons notes, 'legislators appeared more interested in dredging up the shortcomings of wartime aircraft production than in establishing the relationship between the Federal Government and civil aviation', (Komons, 1989, p. 43).

Throughout the 'dark years' for the US aviation industry following the First World War, Samuel Bradley (also head of the Aeronautical Chamber of Commerce formed in January 1922) and others, such as General William 'Billy' Mitchell, stressed the need for the government to finance and manage a revitalization of both the military and commercial sides of the industry, (Komons, 1989, pp. 70-79). Entrepreneurs such as Bill Boeing were in dire need of such help from government. Boeing even put his fledgling enterprise up for sale, but found no takers, losing $300,000 in 1920. But in a move which foreshadowed the future, the company was rescued by government orders for aircraft. In 1921 the Army sought bids for the production of 200 support planes. Boeing won the competition to build them by underbidding even the designer of the plane, Thomas Morse, and then proceeded to make a profit on its manufacture. In the fledgling industry Boeing emerged as the leading supplier of military aircraft, (Rodgers, 1996, p. 35).

A US Strategic Industry

Eventually, industry lobbying in the US began to pay dividends. The efforts of Bradley were finally rewarded as the Morrow Board (appointed by President Coolidge) advised Congress in its report of 30 November 1925 to act in the overseeing of the emerging sector so as to instill public confidence. The result was the Air Commerce Act of 1926, the purpose of which was to regulate and rationalize the airfreight business, give the federal government powers in regulating the safety and licensing of aircraft and pilots, and accompanying five-year procurement plans for both the army and navy. With the act, aviation was thus recognized explicitly as a strategic industry in the United States, (Komons, 1989, p. 88). But the legislation also intended for the Department of Commerce, through its newly-created Aeronautics Branch, to promote the growth of commercial aviation, and in so doing, 'the framers of the Air Commerce Act, by entrusting to a single agency both promotional and regulatory powers, had created a potential and permanent source of conflict', (Komons, 1989, p. 92). Under the direction of the Aeronautics Branch, the federal government was also the driving force behind the creation and maintenance of a network of radio communications and weather information distribution that served as the foundation for subsequent commercial development in aviation.

The Role of Air Mail

Perhaps the most important measure of government help to US commercial aviation had come with the inauguration of air mail service in 1918, which had been followed by the Air Mail Act of 1925 (the Kelly Act) that allowed the awarding of contracts to private concerns for mail delivery, (Komons, p. 66). The economic viability of the new service depended, not only on a network of ground-based navigation capabilities, but also on night flying, and entailed the construction by the Post Office of a network of lighted airways across the country. By so doing, the national government was performing a crucial economic and commercial function relative to the nascent aviation sector: 'In developing its air mail routes, the Post Office, though operating as an arm of the government, was playing the classic role of entrepreneur', (Heppenheimer, 1995, p. 11). Indeed, without its new key role in the service of government, it is doubtful that the industry could have justified its commercial existence:

> Airmail was the only significant civilian application of aircraft. By establishing airfields and installing navigational beacons along its routes ... the Post Office had begun to establish an infrastructure that would allow commercial aviation to expand. Congress hoped to speed up development of passenger and freight service by providing a large, steady airmail business for private airlines, (Rodgers, 1996, p. 36).

There was also federal assistance in the technical sphere. Government support in the form of a wind tunnel built in 1928 by the NACA led to additional and significant technical progress in aircraft design. Used to test the aerodynamic effects of cowling engines by installing them within the wing structure on a aluminum monoplane airframe to reduce drag, 'these developments now offered far-reaching opportunity to design and build a new generation of aircraft that would offer unprecedented speed and performance', (Heppenheimer, 1995, p. 44).

Figure 1.1   Charles Lindbergh (1902-1974)

The solo flight of Charles Lindbergh from New York to Paris in 1927 did more than any single previous event to stimulate public interest in flight and the aviation industry in the United States. His accomplishment created the so-called Lindbergh boom; an explosion of public interest and investment in aviation projects and the firms undertaking them, (Solberg, 1979, p. 73). Lindbergh's popularity provided the public support necessary to allow federal funding of airport construction across the country, in Komons view: 'perhaps the most important promotional activity undertaken by the Aeronautics Branch', (1989, p. 173). The massive influx of capital initiated a period of rapid consolidation and vertical integration within the US aviation industry, with four firms emerging to control virtually all aspects of aircraft production and air travel.

Boeing's Consolidation

The Boeing Company already played a small but significant part in the development of air mail service, flying a batch of mail from Vancouver to Seattle, the first air mail service between the US and Canada. On 3 March 1919, William Boeing and pilot Eddie Hubbard carried the first US international air mail in the Boeing Model C pictured below.

Figure 1.2   Bill Boeing (right) and Eddie Hubbard with a Boeing Model C
Credit: BoeingImages.com

In 1926, two of the company's key employees convinced Bill Boeing to take a substantial risk of his personal capital by building 25 planes to carry the mail and a few passengers along the Chicago-San Francisco segment of the trunk mail routes put up by Congress for bids, (Rodgers, 1996, p. 38). Having won the contract, the Model 40A aircraft would be operated by a new subsidiary incorporated on 17 February 1927 as Boeing Transport Company, carrying not only mail, but a few passengers as well. Involved in both manufacturing aircraft and operating them for commercial purposes, Boeing was now well positioned to respond to the 'Lindbergh boom' in air travel. Taking advantage of investor interest in aviation firms, Bill Boeing listed his company on the New York Stock Exchange on 1 November 1928. He then moved quickly to solidify his market position by merging his holdings with Pratt and Whitney, the Connecticut-based engine manufacturer, creating the United Aircraft and Transport Corporation (UATC) on 1 February 1929. Aggressively pursuing the acquisition of smaller manufacturing concerns and airlines alike, UATC emerged as the country's dominant aeronautics firm by the early 1930s, and Bill Boeing and his partners became millionaires, (the airlines acquired were combined to form United Airlines).

Air Mail Subsidies

The position of Boeing and its counterparts was strengthened further in 1930 when the largest three conglomerates were awarded all but two of the 20 contracts for air mail delivery in the United States. According to Nick Komons, these 'government air mail contracts were in fact lucrative subsidies for carriers', (1989, p. 191). The Air Mail Act of 1930 (McNary-Watres Act) permitted the Postmaster General to grant air mail contracts without competitive bidding, broad powers were adopted, not only to consolidate air mail service but also to encourage mergers among airlines and thus rationalize the industry. By cutting mail rates and paying carriers according to space available, the US government also stimulated the airlines to seek passenger traffic for additional revenue. In so doing the airlines were given a strong spur to technological innovation, as passengers' demands for increased speed and comfort encouraged a wave of innovation in airframe and engine design, (Heppenheimer, 1995, p. 36). Thus, 'By means of this sudden transformation of scale, an industrial base was formed that for the first time put American aviation on an equal footing with European' (Irving, 1993, pp. 31-32).

With the aid of government support and despite the damage done to almost every other sector by the Great Depression, by the early 1930s the aviation conglomerates had become a formidable oligopoly in an industry experiencing rapid structural and technological change. The new economic environment created by the Postal Service, combined with technological changes driven in part by government research facilities, led to the production of planes that could effectively create and then dominate the emerging commercial market.

US Federal Support and the Origin of the Modern Airliner

Further government stimulation to the development of aircraft that would have both military and commercial application came in the form of a US Army contract, which at the time was still flying outmoded biplanes: 'The path to the modern airliner dated from 1929, as Boeing's Claire Egtvedt set out to offer the Army a better bomber', (Heppenheimer, 1995, p. 46). Two design teams at Boeing competed to produce the best solution; the result being the B-9, which 'introduced the twin-engine configuration that would become standard with subsequent airliners', (Heppenheimer, 1995, p. 46). Powered by the new Pratt and Whitney Hornet engines the design was converted into the Boeing 247, of which 60 were promptly ordered by United Aircraft and Transport. The commercial impact was immediate, because with the exclusive right to fly them, 'United could gain a long leg up in the new field of passenger transport', (Heppenheimer, p. 47). The first prototype (the Model 247) flew on 8 February 1933; the twin-engine, all-aluminum monoplane could fly from New York to Los Angeles in under 20 hours, stopping seven times. While seemingly primitive by today's standards, in both appearance and performance, the Boeing 247 was arguably the world's first modern airliner, (Rodgers, 1996, pp. 44-45).

The Rise of Douglas

Despite its impressive technological and commercial achievements, Boeing's conglomerate soon found itself upstaged by a small and previously little-known Californian rival, Donald Douglas. The advantage conferred on United by the B-247 posed serious problems for competitor Transcontinental & Western Air (TWA), later to become better known as Trans World Airways. With Boeing having rejected a request from TWA to buy its new 247 monoplane, as United had exclusive rights to the first 60 produced, in 1932, TWA contacted Donald Douglas, a talented aircraft builder in Los Angeles, about the possibility of a new design for passenger travel. Working along with Jack Northrop, Douglas determined to outstrip the 247 in size and range; the result was the DC-1 prototype, designed around a multicellular wing and a monocoque fuselage, powered by Wright Cyclone engines and fitted with a Hamilton Standard variable-pitch propeller. A model had been tested in the same wind tunnel at Caltech where Boeing had conducted its research on the 247, but the DC-1 also benefited from government research faculties. In fact, the DC-1 'wing's airfoil section was fine-tuned at the laboratories of the National Advisory Committee for Aeronautics, NACA, at Langley in Virginia. NACA also helped to streamline the engine installations', (Irving, 1993, pp. 28-29). Very rapidly the DC-1 metamorphosed into the DC-2 pictured below.

Figure 1.3   Douglas DC-2

The Douglas DC-1 had completed its maiden flight on 1 July 1933, only 332 days after TWA's first approach. But it 'was really a flying laboratory', and was immediately converted into the DC-2, which went into production in direct competition with the Boeing 247, (Irving, 1993, p. 29). TWA ordered 20 DC-2s, which were larger and carried more freight and passengers than the 247. Then, in the summer of 1935, not to be outdone, American Airlines pressed Douglas to enlarge the DC-2 even more. Seeking to capitalize on the 247's relatively small passenger capacity (only ten) Douglas lengthened the fuselage, adopted a larger engine and added wing flaps for greater control on landing. The result was the 21 seat DC-3, 'which could carry more than twice as many passengers as the 247 in far greater comfort, (Irving, 1993, p. 30). The plane was a hit and was even built under license in the USSR: 'Travelers and airlines loved the roomy, economical, technologically superior Douglas airplane, which made the Model 247 obsolete less than a year after its first flight', (Rodgers, 1996, p. 45.) Even United, the original customer for the 247 was compelled to re-equip with DC-3s: 'Within a year, the Douglas airliner was carrying 95 percent of all airline passengers in the United States and 90 percent of all overseas passengers', (Irving, 1993, p. 30).

The Break-up of the Boeing Conglomerate

Even as Boeing faced severe competition in the commercial field, the dissolution of UATC into its component parts (United Airlines, Boeing and Pratt Whitney) took effect on 28 September 1934. The policy of the US Postmaster General, Walter Folger Brown, had backfired. Amidst charges of favouritism toward the larger carriers, whose high profits were widely seen as an abuse of public funds, the existing air mail contracts were cancelled by the Roosevelt administration. In addition, the Aeronautics Branch was recast as the Bureau of Air Commerce, though still within the Commerce Department, (Komons, 1989, p. 240). In conjunction with the new administration's reorganization of governmental supervision of the industry, in 1934 Congress passed the Air Mail Act (Black-McKellar Act), which resurrected competitive bidding for air mail contracts that would henceforth be allocated by the Interstate Commerce Commission (ICC). The legislation also split the aviation business into its two more or less natural halves, manufacturing and transport, by requiring the separation for business purposes of airline manufacturers from aircraft operators, after which many of today's largest airlines were founded as independent entities. Thrown into confusion by this restructuring and suffering from the continuing recession, the manufacturers had not long to wait for more governmental help in the form of authorization for the Army and Navy to purchase 1200 and 2320 planes respectively.

The scandal over the mail contracts impacted very directly on Bill Boeing himself. He became a favourite target during the highly publicized Senate hearings of 1934, concerning the high profits the company had made on the mail contract, and Boeing's personal fortune from stock ownership. Subjected to such indignities, Boeing abruptly quit the business, sold all of his stock in the company, and retired to the life of a country gentleman on his estate. The Boeing Company received only $582,000 in cash, along with the plant and equipment, located mainly around Seattle and in Wichita, Kansas. Claire Egtvedt thus inherited a difficult situation with little work for even the 600 remaining employees, (Rodgers, 1996, p. 49).

Another Military Rescue

In order to find a way out of the mess created by the founder's departure the Boeing Company needed military orders. In May 1934 Egtvedt had thus been very relieved to meet with officials of the Army Air Corps to discuss their secret plans for the experimental design of an extremely large aircraft that would serve as a possible prototype in the development of future bombers. Work on the massive experimental craft continued for some years, and bore fruit in the form of the XB-15, which first flew in 1937, (Rodgers, 1996, p. 54).

Soon after winning the XB-15 contract, Egtvedt was made aware of another competition to design and build an operational bomber, and convinced the firm's board to authorize Boeing engineers to design the B-17 Flying Fortress. Taking advantage of the experimental work already in progress, Boeing flew its newest product to Wright Field in Dayton, Ohio on 20 August 1935, confident of its chances against the designs of its competitors, Douglas and Martin. But the B-17 test flight turned to disaster, as the Air Corps pilots failed to control the huge aircraft's angle of ascent, and the resultant crash killed two onboard. Douglas emerged the winner of an order for 350 bombers (the B-18), yet the Air Corps remained impressed with Boeing's work and ordered 14 B-17s for 'field test' purposes, thus 'keeping Boeing's hopes alive for future production orders', (Rodgers, 1996, p. 54).

In the dark days of the mid-1930s, therefore, it was military work that kept the company afloat, and further established Boeing as a major designer and producer of large aircraft, a key pre-requisite for the company's future commercial success. Indeed, Boeing first sought to convert its expertise in military design and production directly into commercial leverage in negotiations with Pan Am to build a flying boat. Using the design for the XB-15's tail and wing, Boeing submitted the B-314, a proposal for a four engine, two-deck behemoth so radical in its design that Charles Lindbergh, a consultant to Pan Am, advised against accepting. Flown for the first time on 7 June, 1938, the expensive Model 314s – known as Clippers by Pan Am – entered passenger service on the North Atlantic route on 28 June, 1939 but the aircraft's prospects was altered dramatically by the outbreak of war in Europe: 'The Clippers were drafted, requisitioned by the Army and Navy', (Rodgers, p. 56).

Military work led directly to another of Boeing's early commercial products, as alongside the 314, 'the company started on another airliner, a four-engine land plane called the Stratoliner, with a B-17 wing and tail', (Rodgers, p. 56). Egtvedt argued convincingly to TWA and Pan Am that Boeing's experience on the B-17 would allow the rapid development of the new plane, and that it would be a dramatic improvement over the rival Douglas DC-4, able to fly passengers faster, farther and in greater comfort in part because of a pressurized cabin allowing it to cruise above bad weather. However, design flaws were revealed with tragic consequences as representatives of KLM, the Dutch national carrier, were killed along with Boeing's chief engineer in a test flight which went badly wrong in March 1939. Lingering doubts about the aircraft's safety thus limited sales of Stratoliners, which like the Clippers were requisitioned by the US Army.

Creating the Federal Aviation Infrastructure

Franklin D. Roosevelt's first administration had also seen the Federal government enter directly into the control of increasingly busy air traffic, and in June 1936 the Bureau of Air Commerce took over stations at Newark, Chicago and Cleveland, and also designated 73 routes as official civil airways, (Komons, 1989, p. 308). But a series of air disasters in the winter of 1936-1937 forced the resignation of Eugene Vidal and the appointment of Fred Fagg as new director of the Bureau, who re-organized its structure and air traffic procedures. These efforts were not enough to forestall Congressional action on new legislation to broaden the power of the federal government to regulate civil aviation in both its safety and economic dimensions. The result was the McCarran-Lea Act of 1938, which would govern American aviation for the next 20 years, (Komons, p. 379). Under the auspices of the McCarran-Lea Act, the Civil Aeronautics Authority was created to allocate routes and supervise rates, and license carriers. It took over airway regulation from the Bureau of Air Commerce, the setting of air mail rates from the ICC, and air mail routing and scheduling from the Post Office. Several existing airlines received (under a catch-all clause) automatic certification to provide air services, while Pan Am was allowed to retain its near-monopoly position on international routes. Unfortunately, the structure and function of the new Authority repeated past mistakes in that 'combining economic and safety regulation seemed to guarantee a unified policy; there was, however, an inbred conflict of interest in the arrangement that would draw increasingly harsh criticism as the years passed', (Wilson, 1979, p. 11).

Conclusion: the Second World War and Beyond

This chapter has shown how the US Federal government laid the path for the modern American aircraft and aviation industry in the 1920s and 1930s. After the depressed conditions of post-1918, the support of the Federal government for an air mail system, via lucrative contracts and also defense orders for Boeing provided the system, with much needed cash. In a pattern that would be repeated later, Boeing survived lean times on the commercial side because of life-sustaining military orders. The Boeing management also showed great skill in harnessing technology developed via government procurement contracts for use in civil programs.

Figure 1.4   Boeing B-17 Flying Fortress

Boeing benefited significantly from the air strategic policy that the United States pursued in the Second World War. In the 1930s, politicians in Washington saw how Hermann Goerring's Luftwaffe had intimidated Germany's enemies. The US perception of events in Europe in the late 1930s had a profound impact on the emerging consensus for a large and strategically capable airforce. As France and Britain were cowed by Hitler's increasing chauvinism, the view taken in Washington was that Germany's air power was a critical ingredient in the Nazis' ability to bully their European neighbours. While Neville Chamberlain was negotiating the Munich agreement in September 1938, which subsequently became regarded as an infamous act of appeasement, the US ambassador to Germany, William Bullitt, remarked to Roosevelt, 'If you have enough airplanes, you won't have to go to Berchtesgaden', (Quoted, Sherry, 1987, p. 76). According to Roosevelt, Britain had 'cringed like a coward' at Munich' but this was not going to happen to the US.

The means for America to develop an air strategic policy in the early 1930s were designed and created by Boeing in the form of the B-10 and B-17 (Flying Fortress) bombers. The contract for the latter, which had a much-enlarged radius of action than previous planes, was awarded to Boeing in 1933.

Overall, the Second World War provided the US manufacturers with an abundance of riches. During the war the US economy boomed on arms manufacture. In 1940 Roosevelt had called for aircraft production goals of 50,000 planes a year, (Sherry, 1988, p. 91). This was easily surpassed with the US producing in excess of 300,000 aircraft and more than 800,000 aero-engines. As a matter of course, corporations such as Boeing, Douglas, Martin and Lockheed earned enormous profits, (Biddle, 1991, p. 270). Between 1940 and 1945 the United States spent $185 billion on armaments, with a massive $46 billion bill for aviation weapons. Biddle notes, 'In order to win the war the United States spawned a weapons industry of titanic scope', (Biddle, 1991, p. 270).

Boeing developed its main expertise in producing heavy bombers, such as the B-17 and B-29, the last of which delivered the atomic bombs to their targets in 1945. The B-17 Flying Fortress, the most important aircraft in US air strategy for the Pacific theatre, was launched in the mid-1930s when the industry was in the doldrums. But the return of big earnings for Boeing began in earnest in 1938, when mass production of the B-17 started. This emphasis on airpower symbolized a sea change in military affairs; a process had been initiated which would transform the US aircraft industry. In 1939 the industry ranked 41st in output dollar value, in 1944 it was first, (Biddle, 1991, p. 271).

Chapter 2

Boeing and the Cold War: From the Jet Bomber to the Civil Transport

Introduction

During the Second World War, Boeing dominated US military aviation. Boeing's work on heavy bombers also paid dividends later and underpinned its ultimate supremacy in the field of large civil jet manufacture. However, when the production of civil aircraft resumed in earnest after 1945, Douglas was the number one manufacturer, challenged by Lockheed. Both companies produced reliable four-engine airliners, developed from types conceived in the late 1930s and early 1940s, which they depended on to maintain their position and to establish their post-war product line. But as this chapter illustrates future success in the market required a new technology.

Figure 2.1   **Douglas DC-3**

During the Second World War the key technological advance in aeronautical engineering was the development of the gas turbine engine in Britain and Germany, which was to become the key factor on which the British were to rely to challenge the industry's leaders in the US. The turbo-prop powered British Vickers Viscount flew in 1948, but this was a sideshow compared to the arrival in 1949 of the first jet airliner to enter airline service, the de Havilland Comet; another first for British aeronautics.

Figure 2.2   The British de Havilland Comet IV

Britain's pioneering entry into the civil jet market was the de Havilland Comet, a jet aircraft of complex and advanced design, which was years ahead of its time. If it had not been for a fatal flaw associated with metal fatigue, it might have established the United Kingdom as the world's leading manufacturer of large civil jet aircraft.

The years 1952-59 were decisive in the evolution of civil air transport. They were also years of rapid technological advance. The Comet 1, which went into service in 1952, flew higher and faster than many front-line military fighters of the time. Douglas and Lockheed had existing piston-engine product lines to defend, and one stream of thought held that aircraft performance would remain almost unchanged, but that the gas turbine, driving a propeller, would eventually replace the piston engine. Military freighters built by Douglas, from the C-124 Globemaster to the C-133 Cargomaster, followed this reasoning, and small numbers were ordered by the USAF. Lockheed's first turbine powered airliner was the L-188 Electra, which first flew in 1958. The Electra was designed to compete with the successful Vickers Viscount, which preceded it by some 10 years. The Electra met technical problems and production was stopped after 172 had been sold; a military version, the Orion maritime patrol aircraft, remained in production for over 20 more years and over 650 were delivered. But steadily Lockheed's position in civil aviation declined and the 1960s saw no new Lockheed civil projects enter production. In the meantime Boeing's ability to spin-off defense technology into civil applications and its astute political awareness allowed it to push Douglas into second place.

The Geo-Political Context and Boeing's Dominance in the Civil Sector

During the Second World War and the early stages of the Cold War, the technological and organizational capabilities of the United States were definitive of its military, economic and political status as a superpower. With the formidable design and production capabilities of the USSR devoted mainly to military purposes and confined to the Communist bloc, with Japan lacking an independent capability in aeronautics, and remaining during this period very much America's military and diplomatic client, the US was the world's pre-eminent aeronautical power. By the end of the 1950s American aircraft would define the technological and organizational frontier of both military and commercial aeronautics. Defense contractors were able to apply their military technology to the business of commercial manufacturer; doubling as commercial manufacturers they incorporated airframes, propulsion and flight-control systems developed for military use into civilian products, while selling both types of goods into the vast and uncontested US market.

The Legacy of the Second World War

In the US, tremendous increases in productive capacity were attained during the Second World War. The US aeronautics industry workforce of fewer than 49,000 in 1939 grew to over 2.1 million in 1943. The Boeing Company mirrored this wider process as its workforce grew from just 4000 in 1939 to 30,000 in 1943, largely because of demand for B-17s, (Sabbagh, 1996, p. 29). Branch plants, licensee and subcontractor arrangements were all used to create the necessary production and assembly space; the major airframe and engine builders became primarily designers and assemblers of parts and sections built elsewhere, as labour and capital were effectively combined. From January 1940 to the Japanese surrender in August 1945, US manufacturers produced some 300,317 military aircraft. Boeing profited handsomely on the back of wartime contracts: 'In the five years the United States was in the war, 1941-1945, the company made an astounding profit of $27,579,864, an average of over $5.5m per year', (Rodgers, 1995, p. 66). Today this profit would be equivalent to US$284m or US$58m per year.

But unit numbers alone mask the importance of the continual increases in aircraft size and weight, which meant that much of the new productive capacity, in terms of tools, skills and organization alike, literally had to be invented on the shop floor. Flexibility and coordination were the watchwords in descending steep production learning curves. Weight of output per employee increased from 21 pounds in January 1941 to 96 pounds in August 1944, while the cost of producing a four-engine, long-range bomber fell from US$15.18 to US$4.82 per pound, (Simonson, 1968, pp. 161-178).

Ironically, Boeing and the other manufacturers of war material were the victims of their own success, in that their skill and dedication in producing the instruments so effective in defeating the Axis powers, threatened to put them all out of a job. The cessation of hostilities in 1945 brought a drastic, if predictable, drop in the level of government orders that had so dramatically expanded and transformed the US aviation industry. Although winding down for some time already, 90% of existing contracts, totaling over US$9 billion, were summarily cancelled in that year alone. Industry sales fell from US$16m in 1944 to US$1.2m in 1947.

Cold War Industrial Policy

The impact of the post-war cutbacks on Boeing and its workers was especially devastating, as the company had been engaged in maximum production right up to the end of the war, forcing the immediate layoff of thousands of workers in Washington and Kansas, (Rodgers, 1995, p. 80). Just as had been the case following the First World War, Boeing's management scrambled to find non-aircraft-related businesses to enter, but to little avail. A degree of success was realized in converting to commercial use Boeing's work on the C-97 Stratofreighter, a transport developed for the Army Air Force (AAF) and based on the B-29. Dubbed the Stratocruiser, the double-deck airliner made its first flight on 8 July 1947, with Pan Am as the launch customer. However, only 50 were built, entering service with US airlines and the British flag carrier BOAC.

Figure 2.3   Boeing C-97 Stratofreighter

But US fears of repeating the disorderly contraction in government orders after the First World War that had been so damaging to the industry were not to be realized, because both international politics and the conduct of warfare had been changed irrevocably in the interim, (Vander Muelen, p. 188). Even as Boeing and the other American airframers sought commercial opportunities, the American military was preparing to transform the entire industry in response to the challenges of the early Cold War. Key members of the US military elite in the United States recognized what their German and Japanese counterparts knew all too well: that American air power had been decisive in defeating the Axis. Even before the promulgation of the Truman Doctrine and the signing of the National Security Act, plans had been laid by General Henry H. 'Hap' Arnold, General George C. Marshall (then US Army Chief of Staff) and others to change the whole status of airpower. This recognition of the impact of airpower in the war was the key factor in the decision to remove the air forces from under the army's direct control. Among the many important provisions of the National Security Act of 1947 was the creation of the United States Air Force (USAF), under the newly formed National Military Establishment, later the Department of Defense. Colonel William 'Billy' Mitchell's long-standing dream of air forces as a separate and equal military service arm was finally a reality.

The enhancement of the status of air power within the US military was reinforced by the December 1947 report of the Finletter Commission, entitled 'Survival in the Air Age', which concluded that United States military strategy should be based primarily on air power. Included were recommendations to increase substantially the strength of the air arm, ideas that General Curtis LeMay, appointed head of the newly created Strategic Air Command in October 1948, was quick to champion. Events only confirmed the validity of these views; indeed, the situation in Berlin provided a challenge that seemingly could be met only through the effective application of air power. The Soviet blockade of land, rail and water access into Berlin prompted the US military governor of Germany, General Lucius Clay, to recall General Tunner's success in supplying the nationalist Chinese in the Second World War, and thus initiate, in partnership with the British, an unprecedented airlift to supply the beleaguered city in June 1948. General Curtis LeMay, then commander of US forces in Europe, was quick to respond with around-the-clock transport capability, which delivered provisions in the face of Soviet harassment. The supply of the city throughout the winter and the Soviets' eventual abandonment of their adventure on 12 May 1949 were crucial, not only in creating confidence in the American commitment to Berlin, Germany, Europe and the defense of the West, but also in establishing the importance and credibility of the USAF.

The Market Impact of the Cold War

The new reliance on air power in assuring national security meant that the newest of the armed services would take the lead in issuing large, long-term contracts to firms for the development and manufacture of what had now become expensive and complex weapons systems. Through the procurement practices of the air force, the political and military leadership of the United States exerted strong influence on both sides of the aeronautics' market, providing not only final demand for the products, but also insuring the industry a steady stream of research and development (R&D) financing. After the triumph of the Berlin Airlift, events continued to conspire to encourage an increasing US reliance on air power for both strategic deterrence and tactical capability. The explosion of a Soviet nuclear device in August 1949 confirmed the need for the US military to maintain and improve its ability to deliver atomic weapons into the heart of the USSR.

Reliance on the new jet technology was given further impetus by the outbreak of war on the Korean peninsula, especially over the feared 'MiG Alley', where Soviet MiG-15s demonstrated formidable power and agility. The Korean conflict provided an especially dramatic fillip to the industry: 'the Pentagon's spending on the aerospace industry shot up from $2.6 billion in 1950 to $10.6 billion in 1954', (Sampson, 1977, p. 99). In fact, for the 1945 to 1969 period, 'the defense portion of total R&D expenditures never fell below 65 percent', (Mowery and Rosenberg, 1982, pp. 101-161) and during that period the Air Force spent over 70% of its funds on product development.

Taken together, the rapid changes in the nature of the post-war threat and the technological responses to that challenge meant that US military planners became enmeshed in a procurement process involving the research, design and development of highly complex industrial products. It was the interaction of the imperatives of the international situation, as perceived by the US political and military leadership, and the technological and organizational characteristics of the aeronautical industry, that provided the impetus for eventual American dominance of this crucial economic sector. Along with the rapid development of a massive industrial capability built on an extensive subcontractor base, the procurement of expensive and complex military aircraft also developed exceptionally tight links between government and industry in contract administration. Indeed, the US government had in effect a de-facto industrial policy toward the aeronautics sector. Under the intense geopolitical pressures of the Cold War the air force could not rely on market forces alone to secure the technology necessary to deter Soviet aggression. National security had become equated with industrial policy, (Hooks, 1991, p. 235).

The Cold War: Translating Military Imperatives into Commercial Advantage

The impact of government procurement policies was to be felt far beyond the core of the emerging military-industrial complex. The nature of the technologies and manufacturing processes in aeronautics insured that the effects of government research and procurement policies would be felt in related sectors on both the military and commercial sides of the industry. The development and construction of modern aircraft require the assembly of several subsystems that are extremely complex and whose successful integration is made even more difficult by their highly interactive nature. Propulsion systems, aerodynamics engineering, construction materials and guidance systems are only the most obvious examples of the large number of distinct industrial sectors stimulated by the inherently eclectic nature of aircraft design and manufacture. As observed in a major study on the impact of military procurement policies on the economic geography of the United States:

> The cold war initiated a new era of industrial progress, nourished by government-financed, military-led research and development, with guaranteed government markets. The new dominant industries, arrayed around the aerospace complex, faced qualitatively new demands; to make small batches of experimental or innovative gear, with disproportionate numbers of scientists and engineers and dwindling numbers of blue-collar workers, (Markusen et. al, p. 230).

Since 'the history of technical development in commercial aircraft consists largely of the utilization for commercial purposes of technical knowledge developed for military purposes at government expense', (Mowery and Rosenberg, p. 140), the effects of the massive government R&D effort were transmitted rapidly into the civilian arena. By converting funding and expertise gained on military contracts to civilian applications, certain US firms, principally Boeing, were able to derive products that would effectively create entirely new markets as their use was adopted. Not that American firms were ready to rely solely on the emerging market for mass civilian air travel made possible by the new technology; profitable military sales remained crucial sources of capital and innovation for future product development. Neither did they intend to confine themselves to the US domestic defense market; pressure on their European competitors was intensified as the US government stepped up its efforts to sell overseas weapons developed for its own use. Used both as a means of extending political influence in the Cold War contest and to lower the unit cost of increasingly complex and expensive systems, stiff American competition compelled European manufacturers 'to set initial prices which would require sales of 250 to 350 aircraft in order to reach the break-even point', (Hochmuth, 1974, p. 152). Having themselves long resorted to intense overseas sales campaigns to reduce procurement costs to their own armed services, the French and British governments and manufacturers alike found their traditional markets in Asia and the Middle East targeted by US producers who benefited in their sales efforts from substantial Pentagon support, (Bright, p. 15).

Firms, quick to capitalize on the translation of capital, technology and production process knowledge into commercial ventures, could position themselves and their products at a crucial nexus connecting the military and economic domains of national security. The intensity of Cold War conflict was decisive in transforming the technological and organizational features of the US aviation industry, not least because it 'marked the watershed between piston and jet production', (Constant, 1980). More than any of its rivals, Boeing's post-war commercial fortunes would ultimately depend on research and development work done for the AAF involving the era's revolutionary aeronautical technology, the jet engine. The military situation at the time had made the development of an indigenous American capacity in jet propulsion imperative, and the various US airframe manufacturers were the direct beneficiaries of the military crisis.

Despite all of its advantages in simplicity of design and the accompanying savings in power to weight ratios and aerodynamic efficiency, the development of the jet engine was perhaps the single most important factor behind the rapid increases in the complexity and cost of developing new aircraft. Deceptively straightforward in their method of providing thrust, jet engines require unparalleled materials integrity and engineering exactitude for successful operation. With actual performance not readily predictable from design projections, frequent and exhaustive testing followed by reworking was required, with the emphasis always on peak performance and flawless reliability, (Constant, 1980).

Like their counterparts at other firms, Boeing engineers were aware of the theoretical possibility of jet propulsion but had been surprised to see it in operation in March 1943. Summoned to Muroc (later Edwards) Air Base in the Mojave desert by AAF officials, Wellwood Beall and his Boeing colleagues, along with representatives of other American aeronautical firms had witnessed US history, as the XP-59, an experimental aircraft built by Bell and powered by General Electric jet engines based on a design by Frank Whittle, took off and flew overhead.

Tasked by the AAF with investigating the military potential of such innovative aircraft, the various engineering teams proceeded to develop prototypes, and Boeing's version was designated the B-47. But, as Rodgers notes, 'At that point, although Boeing realized it dimly if at all, and the government, military, and other manufacturers hadn't a clue, the race was on for supremacy in the business of making commercial jet airplanes', (Rodgers, p. 93).

Integrating the Jet Engine with the B-47 Airframe

Boeing was especially well positioned to conduct research on the new technology, having earlier been convinced of the wisdom of constructing its own state-of-the-art wind tunnel, capable of simulating air speeds verging on the speed of sound. The decision to build it had entailed significant risk, as at the time the company was in debt to the tune of US$3.4m. Boeing had issued new stock and also arranged a loan of US$5.5 billion from the Reconstruction Finance Corporation to fund the venture. The go-ahead for the tunnel was given in August 1941, and having come on line in February 1944, 'Boeing engineers immediately put the tunnel to use in designing the B-47, running it day and night', (Rodgers, p. 95). Once operational, the tunnel was relatively cheap to operate, one of the few times Boeing's geographical location had proved a competitive advantage. The main expense of operating the tunnel after its construction was electric power, which, after the damming of the Columbia river 'was a third or less what it was anywhere else in the United States' (Irving, p. 48). Boeing combined its advantages effectively, using the facility to steal a march on its competition in jet aircraft design, which would prove insurmountable: 'The tunnel was the great enabler. It gave Boeing six times the wind tunnel time available to any competitor', (Irving, p. 88).

Engineers at Boeing were therefore among the first to confront head on the theoretical and practical implications of the jet engine for powered flight. Based in part on the results obtained from tests on the prototype conducted in the wind tunnel, they discovered that significant modifications to existing airframe design would be necessary to accommodate the aerodynamic properties of jet-powered flight. Their suspicions (unpopular as these were with AAF officials, concerned primarily with bringing the new technology to practical application as rapidly as possible) were confirmed by George Schairer, the chief aerodynamicist for Boeing, and Hugh Dryden, later head of the National Aeronautics & Space Administration (NASA). The two men had been part of an intelligence team in Germany at the time of the surrender in May 1945, tasked to examine the Nazi research archives on jet flight, an area in which the Germans had possessed a demonstrated superiority by the end of the war. Examination of captured diagrams and drawings, along with visits to a Messerschmitt factory, revealed dramatic departures in airframe design; wings and horizontal tail surfaces swept back 45% and engines mounted in pods, suspended below the wings.

The Benefits of German Technology

Recognizing the potential importance of these discoveries for the B-47 project, Schairer had sent drawings and notes of his impressions to Seattle, where the B-47 design team immediately began to test the new design in the tunnel, (Rodgers, 1995, p. 98). With the safe arrival of Schairer's urgent communication from Germany, Boeing engineers realized the full significance that the rapid and effective application of such a design might have for the company, (Irving, p. 83). Within a week of receiving Schairer's letter, Boeing engineers had a crude swept wing in the tunnel, and 'at once they could see the significance for the XB-47', (Irving, p. 86). The radical wing would allow the plane to approach closer than ever to the speed of sound, and with speed came improved fuel-efficiency and increased range: 'The swept wing would render the jet engine more efficient at the bomber's optimum performance', (Irving, p. 87). Therefore, armed with top-secret military information and equipped with the industry's most advanced test facilities, Boeing established itself as the vanguard of the jet age: 'Right at the start, Boeing jumped out to a lead it never relinquished, using revolutionary development techniques and producing a design that was radically different from the designs of its competitors', (Rodgers, 1996, p. 93).

The advantages of being first mover were not immediately apparent, as incorporation of these design changes necessarily slowed the development of Boeing's prototype, which was not rolled out until 12 September, and did not complete its first successful flight until 17 December 1947. Because of the radically new and unpredictable handling and performance characteristics, the test flight program was frustratingly slow, but also dangerous; in one instance even deadly. In its primitive state, the swept wing could not be controlled in flight, even in the tunnel, a problem compounded by uncertainty as to the proper location for the jet engines on the aircraft. Trial and error revealed a practical, if aesthetically inelegant solution; putting the engines under the wings on pods that allowed the flow of air into and around the engines in relative independence of the wing. To further complicate matters, such a solution raised new problems of structural design, as the wing would require sufficient flexibility to handle the aerodynamic forces created by the engines mounted underneath. But as fortune would have it, and continued experimentation would reveal, locating the pods properly tended to dampen the tendency of the wing to pitch upward suddenly and violently. By trial and error, a workable configuration for a jet aircraft was emerging, 'The interplay of the flexible wing and the leverage generated by the engine pods acted like an immanent control system ... a breathtakingly sophisticated solution, once realized, but it had been arrived at in a strikingly unsophisticated way', (Irving, p. 93).

These improvisational adjustments to the new reality of near-sonic jet-powered flight added up to a radically novel design for an aircraft, and one that was as yet far from proven. This was a fact tragically underscored by the death of the son of Sir Geoffrey de Havilland in September 1946 while flight-testing the British DH-108 experimental jet, (Irving, p. 96).

Under the skilled and daring hand of test pilot Tex Johnston, B-47 flight-testing progressed rapidly, and the tests vindicated both the radical design and the patience of the AAF. Boeing was rewarded with a rush contract for production of ten of the jet bombers in September 1948, just as the Berlin Airlift was intensifying, (Rodgers, 1995, p. 111).

Figure 2.4   Boeing B-47

Production began in January 1950 in Wichita rather than Seattle (a very controversial decision forced upon Boeing by the Air Force), and under the pressure of the Korean War the company was compelled to help both Douglas and Lockheed build the B-47, of which 2,040 of its various types were eventually delivered, (Rodgers, 1995, p. 110).

The B-47 program epitomized the symbiotic nature of the relationship between the Cold War priorities of the US government, as manifest in the procurement policies of the AAF and USAF, and the capabilities of the country's leading aeronautical manufacturers, with Boeing as the prime example. The ability to design and build the aircraft itself was not the only advantage gained by Boeing from the innovative military program. Through its role in the project, 'Boeing was not simply proving the serviceability of a bomber. The plane had become the triggering spore in the breeding process of the company's next generation of aircraft – military and commercial', (Rodgers, 1995, p. 111).

In June 1946, the AAF had commissioned Boeing to design a long-range, heavy-duty bomber, but the contract specified that it be powered by turboprops, a sort of hybrid of the new pure jet and the traditional propeller engines. Boeing had tried hard to make the design work, but was informed on 21 October 1948 by the Air Force contract officer that the proposed design was unsatisfactory and that there would be an entirely new competition for a jet-powered machine.

Figure 2.5   Boeing B-52

Chief aerodynamicist George Schairer asked if Boeing might not be allowed to keep the contract if they could come up with a convincing proposal for such a design in a hurry, in fact over the weekend. Assembling a crack crew and working in a hotel suite, Schairer presented the formal proposal (complete with balsawood model) to Colonel Warden in his office at Wright field; an initiative which allowed Boeing to retain the contract. This feat was possible because Boeing had already been doing preliminary design work for the Air Force on the B-55, a jet bomber even more sophisticated than the B-47, and in the suite at the Van Cleve hotel, many of those ideas were incorporated in the proposal.

The first flight took place on 15 April 1952 and eventually 744 B-52s were built before production ceased in 1962. As was the case on the B-47 project, Boeing developed many competencies in this defense work that would also have commercial applications. So although the B-55 was never built, 'as it was reincarnated as the B-52 its design introduced ideas that took Boeing much closer to what it would need as a jetliner', (Irving, p. 114). Thus, insights and skills derived from the B-47 were most directly and immediately applied by Boeing to the development of the eight-engine B-52, which also helped Boeing on the path to commercial jets such as the 707.

The Dash 80, the KC-135 and the 707

In the race to build the world's first jet passenger planes in the early 1950s, transatlantic rivalry intensified the pressure for decisive action and raised the stakes of success or failure. The threat of the de Havilland Comet was a timely reminder of European capability and pushed Boeing and the other American airframers towards seeking active support from the US government. Lobbying through the Aircraft Industry Association (AIA) came to nothing, and neither could any of the airlines be convinced to risk their own funds by committing in advance to buy a civil jet transport.

Given their experience with the B-47, Boeing's engineers and management were uniquely positioned to respond to the challenge posed by Europe and, especially at that time, the UK. But the company was divided about the advisability of launching such an ambitious project with uncertain commercial prospects. Perceptions shifted decisively in favour of the commercial potential of the jet transport as Boeing President Bill Allen finally flew on a B-47 in Wichita in August 1950, the same summer he witnessed the Comet in flight at the Farnborough air show, (Rodgers, 1995, p. 155). Financial factors also played a role in Allen's ultimate decision to begin development of a new jet transport, as the company found itself on an exceptionally firm footing, (Rodgers, p. 157).

But ultimately it was concern for the company's very future as a builder of commercial aircraft that drove the momentous decision, (Rodgers, p. 159). Allen's strategy was an ingenious one, designed to capture both military and civilian business, but undertaken in such a way that the military contract would cover most if not all of the investment. Allen determined that Boeing should design and build a jet transport that would serve as a prototype for both a military in-flight refueling aircraft and a commercial airliner. If all went according to plan, Boeing could produce the tanker first, and if and when 'the Air Force placed an order, Boeing could recover much of its heavy investment in the prototype from Independent Research and Development funds', (Rodgers, p. 161). Allen then hoped to convince the Air Force to approve use of the tanker tooling for producing the airliner, for which the government would receive a fee but still leave room for handsome profits.

Boeing's board of directors gave its approval on 20 May 1952 to Allen's project, which had been designated the 707. Design and production would take place at the facilities in Renton, the government-owned factory that had built the B-29. Since the prototype would be pitched first to the military, Allen decided to drop the 707 moniker during the early stages of its development and instead call the aircraft the Model 367-80, a designation consistent with past military projects such as the C-97 transport and the KC-97 tanker. Therefore, within Boeing the program was referred to as the Dash 80 and its commercial significance downplayed in public communications. The first prototype was rolled out in May 1954 with even Bill Boeing, the company's founder, in attendance, and nearly nine years to the day since George Schairer's notes and drawings from the Messerschmitt factory had arrived. Few outside Boeing itself appreciated the significance of the accomplishment. One notable exception was the head of Rolls-Royce, Lord Hives, who was shown the plane by Schairer and, in the wake of the Comet crashes declared the Dash 80 'the end of British aviation'.

Figure 2.6   Boeing Model 367-80 (Dash 80)

Configured as a tanker, the Dash 80 underwent taxi tests until Boeing's chief test pilot Tex Johnston took it on a dramatic first flight in July 1954, an event covered heavily by the media; *Time* magazine even featured Bill Allen on its cover. The aircraft owed so much in design and process technology to the military version that the original prototype rolled out in Seattle had no windows in the fuselage. In March 1955, Allen's strategy was vindicated as the Pentagon announced that the KC-135, the military tanker version of the Dash 80, would be bought from Boeing instead of Lockheed. In July 1955, Allen convinced the Air Force that, for a fee, Boeing could use the tooling and factory space dedicated to the KC-135 for production of a commercial jetliner. Even though the physical infrastructure to handle jet transports was lacking, 'all Allen could do was to plow ahead and trust that jetliners would prove so attractive that the world would have to catch up', (Rodgers, 1995, p. 177).

A Challenge from Douglas

The Dash 80 did not translate directly into its commercial version. Learning of the Dash 80 through Charles Lindbergh, Juan Trippe of Pan American pressed Douglas to develop a jetliner, to be called the DC-8, on which development began in June 1955. Even though his engineers could simply copy the main design feature of the Dash 80, Donald Douglas faced formidable technological obstacles that translated into substantial commercial risk: 'With no prototype, he'd have to go straight into production, whereas Boeing in effect would have two prototypes with the Dash 80 and the KC-135. The DC-8 had to make or break itself in the commercial market, while Boeing had the military market as a cushion with its tanker version. The Douglas company would have to pay all development and production costs itself, while the military would be sharing many costs with Boeing', (Rodgers, p. 177). Douglas rose to the challenge, and in doing so confronted Boeing's Bill Allen with a formidable problem. Rather ironically, Douglas held a number of advantages by starting late and having no firm engineering plans or production capability in place.

Figure 2.7   Douglas DC-8

Douglas's products still dominated the civil market, and, using its detailed knowledge of customer requirements, it had designed the DC-8 with a fuselage three inches larger in diameter than the 707. Douglas also adopted Juan Trippe's proposal that the DC-8 incorporate a larger and more powerful Pratt and Whitney engine, the JT4, which was then under development. This would allow the Douglas jetliner to fly non-stop on transcontinental and transatlantic routes, thereby making the 707 obsolete before it had flown. In its original incarnation the Boeing product had demonstrated appeal to none of the airlines, and United had just given an order to Douglas for DC-8s. 'For Allen, the trauma was not just a financial nightmare. As well as anyone in the company, he remembered the ignominy of the Boeing 247 and the DC-3', (Irving, p. 155). Allen's worst fears were realized as Pan Am announced a decision on 13 October 1955 to split its initial order for jet aircraft between Boeing and Douglas; 20 707s and 25 DC-8s. Furthermore, Pan Am informed Boeing that the 707s were being purchased only so the airline could claim to be the first to offer jet service, but that the 707s would be replaced by DC-8s as soon as practicable. United Airlines followed suit on 25 October with an order for 30 DC-8s and no 707s, citing the superior cabin space promised by the Douglas fuselage.

American Airlines was the next carrier scheduled to announce its purchase decision, and Allen instructed his engineers to prepare a proposal for an aircraft larger and longer than either the 707 or the DC-8, and built around a redesigned wing. Although a major departure from the initial concept derived from both the Dash 80 and the KC-135, Allen felt that the new 707 Intercontinental was well worth the technological and financial risk. A working prototype did exist, and the tanker had been bought by the military. Allen's commercial instincts proved sound, as American Airlines boss C.R. Smith announced on 8 November 1955 that he would order no DC-8s, and Pan Am soon after cancelled its order with Douglas and opted for the improved 707; 'Winning the American order, as far as domestic airlines were concerned, was the turning point for the 707. For the moment, at least, it was still a two-horse race', (Irving, p. 156). A further huge boost was given to the Boeing sales campaign when President Eisenhower ordered three 707s for use by the Executive branch, thus making Boeing the builder of Air Force One.

Figure 2.8   Boeing 707

The redesigned 707 made its first flight on 20 December 1957, again with the redoubtable Tex Johnston at the controls, approximately 18 months after its sister craft, the KC-135 tanker. US certification followed. However, because it was such a radically new aircraft 'rather than designing FAA regulations into the 707, they found themselves recasting FAA rules to encompass the 707', (Irving, p. 162). Although the 707 flew safely, its operators, especially Pan Am, were far from satisfied with its performance in terms of range and payload. Pan Am would buy a few 707s as they were, but would also buy even more DC-8s, and expected the 707 to be improved. Boeing engineers understood the root of the problem: 'It was the wing; it simply wasn't big enough', (Irving, pp. 162-163).

Making a virtue of necessity, Boeing engineers perceived 'a golden opportunity to distill everything Boeing now knew about swept wings into something like an optimum … the wing underwent an almost fluid and immensely subtle series of changes in profile', (Irving, p. 165). Within six weeks, the redesign was complete, and when fitted with Pratt and Whitney's latest fanjet, the JT-4, the 707-320B (as the new model was called) 'was so good that Pan Am went on buying them, in batch after batch', (Irving, p. 167). By effectively deploying expertise gained by meeting the Air Force's demands for jet-propelled implements of war, Boeing had established itself firmly in the commercial realm. The gamble of the Dash 80 had worked, and Boeing and its 707 would indeed be definitive of the term 'jet age'. 'In October 1958, when a Pan Am 707 left New York for its first scheduled flight to Paris, it could carry nearly 60 more people than a Stratocruiser and cruise almost twice as fast, at a altitude 70 percent greater than the average propeller plane of the day, well above the onerous weather', (Irving, p. 173).

Other Competitors

Detailed design work on the de Havilland Comet began in 1946 and it first flew in July 1949. Like most British large jet aircraft of the period, the four turbojets were mounted within the wings close to the fuselage rather than in underwing pods. The aircraft began commercial operations in 22 January 1952, with a maiden flight to Johannesburg. The Comet was a huge advance on existing airliners and flew nearly twice as fast as its competitors. But the commercial potential of the British plane was undermined by a structural flaw.

The first sign of a key safety defect in the Comet came on 2 May 1953 when one crashed after take-off from Calcutta. Two more crashes occurred in 1954. As no obvious explanation for the accidents was to be found, the entire fleet was grounded for investigation. In February 1955 it was confirmed that the relatively unknown phenomenon of metal fatigue was the problem. After thousands of pressurized climbs and descents the metal around the Comet's square windows became prone to cracking, eventually causing sudden and catastrophic depressurization.

Figure 2.9   de Havilland Comet IV

The existing Comets were either scrapped or modified but the redesigned Comet IV did not re-enter airline service until 1958, by which time the battle with the US had been lost. The interruption to commercial service and the damage to the aircraft and manufacturer's reputation meant that the British challenger to Boeing and Douglas failed.

In the midst of intensifying competition with Douglas, Boeing also faced a technological and commercial challenge from another American company, Convair; a company that also had extensive experience designing and building aircraft for the military. Responding with alacrity to the possibility of a market for smaller jet transports, Convair attempted to fill the niche with its own jetliner, the 880. Sensing the possible emergence of a serious new competitor, in 1956 Boeing dealt the commercial ambitions of Convair a major blow by successfully pitching at the last minute a variant of the 707 to United Airlines, killing off an order for 28 880s (Allen was forced to designate the new derivative 720 instead of 717 because United's Pat Patterson would not buy an airplane with two sevens in its name). Then in early 1958, Boeing snatched a large portion of an order to American Airlines that Convair hoped to reap with its 990 jetliner.

The sales competition took on added significance, as the modified Convair aircraft was built around a new engine designed and built by General Electric called a fan jet, in which a fan enclosed in a nacelle on the front of the engine acted as a form of propeller. Realizing that the new technology promised increases in power, speed and range and thus offered substantial economies of operation, Bill Allen pressed Pratt and Whitney to develop a similar engine to fit the Boeing 720. He then presented the package to American Airline's executives (again at the last minute), who split their order between the two companies. While both aircraft demonstrated the effectiveness of the fan jet technology, the 720 proved so superior to the 990 that Convair was eliminated as a force in the market for commercial jet aircraft, leaving Boeing and Douglas as the only two serious American contenders, (Rodgers, p. 171). Pan Am flew the first regularly scheduled commercial service of a 707 on 26 October 1958 from New York to Paris, and the DC-8 made its first commercial flight in September 1959.

In a further ironic twist which demonstrated clearly the power of airline executives to determine the fortunes of the airframers C. R. Smith, the CEO of American Airlines, encouraged Lockheed to develop a turboprop airliner, the Electra, which as the launch customer American put into service in early 1959. But the aircraft suffered from structural problems and sold only a total of 176, losing Lockheed millions of dollars.

Douglas Falters

As we have seen, it was initially possible that Douglas aircraft could have eclipsed Boeing in the 1950s. However, not only did Boeing's redesign of the 707 neutralise the threat from the DC-8, Douglas also failed to expand its product line as quickly as its Seattle competitor. It was not until 1963 that Douglas launched another new product, the twin-engine DC-9, which entered service in December 1965. The DC-9 was delayed because of a financial crisis in the company caused by its continuous failure in USAF competitions, (Norris and Wagner, 2001, p. 27). Ultimately, the DC-9 was a sales success, but also something of a financial disaster, as the production system was quite unable to cope with the rush of orders. Offering different variants in different markets enhanced sales appeal, but added to the glitches in production.

As we can see in table 2.1 below Boeing won out in the 1950s competition for supremacy in first-generation civil jets. The rapid redesign of the 707 in response to airline criticism and its dual use role as a tanker ensured domination for Boeing.

Table 2.1   Sales of First Generation Civil Jets

Type	Civil	Military
de Havilland Comet (all versions)	112	
Boeing 707	1010	820
Douglas DC-8	556	
Convair 880/990	102	

Boeing was also helped by its rival's self-inflicted wounds. The problems on the DC-9 were the first symptoms of a lack of effective communication between Douglas' Sales and Production staff that would plague the company for a quarter of a century. The classic Douglas failure lay in the fact that Sales and Marketing would do deals involving deadlines and prices, which Production could not deliver on. With declining profits from military sales, the civil aircraft production side never obtained the investment to enable its efficiency to approach that of Boeing. Douglas's inability to deliver on time cost the company a great deal, both financially and in reputation. The problem of the inter-relationships between Design, Production and Marketing/Sales were solved eventually, but too late to save the company from first, the merger with McDonnell in 1967 and second, the absorption by Boeing 30 years later. In 1998 the name of Douglas aircraft disappeared forever.

The Benefits of Dual Production

Jet airliners revolutionized the air travel business, at once making flight cheaper, faster and more pleasurable, with the only negative aspects being noise and jet lag. A new phase in the history of aeronautics had opened, with implications extending far beyond the industry itself. With the commercial jet, travel by plane would be within the financial reach of millions, and it was a Boeing aircraft that had literally defined the emerging business. As Rodgers notes, 'A mass commercial air-travel market didn't exist before the pioneering Boeing [707] jetliner', (1996, p. 202). Capitalizing on its experience as a military contractor during the Second World War and the crucial early phases of the Cold War, especially on the B-47 project, Boeing had created a new commercial environment and thus set the ground rules under which future competition would take place.

The key to all this was the 707. However, the point at which the 707 became profitable to Boeing is a matter of conjecture, and a precise calculation would depend on internal accounting practices and rely on proprietary data available only to the company. Nevertheless, it is clear that the dual development of a civil and defense product was critical to Boeing's commercial success. As we have shown a key advantage for the US manufacturers has been the synergies that exist between defense and civil aerospace technologies. This was noted in an authoritative Congressional Office of Technology Assessment study published in 1991. While the study analyses the support systems of other countries, it also recognizes Federal support for US manufacturers. As the author notes:

> The single greatest means by which US government policy has affected the competitiveness of the commercial aircraft industry is in the procurement of military aircraft and funding of the related R&D ... In some cases whole systems developed for the military have been "spun off" to commercial applications, reducing development costs and risks to the commercial users, (COTA, 1991, p. 30).

Defense contracts help to alleviate conditions in the aircraft industry, which make profitability difficult to achieve. The huge development costs of aircraft make a large program essential if profit is to be realized. Defense sales ease the burden when commercial production has not reached the minimum efficiency of scale necessary for a particular aircraft's production run. Similarly, contrasting commercial and defense cycles offer potential buffers against market downturns. In the early 1990s chairman Frank Schrontz acknowledged the benefits that the military contracts had brought, '[A] defense-commercial mix provides long-term stability and a testing ground for new technologies lacking immediate commercial application. Financially there have been times when the defense side carried the commercial business', (Quoted, *Wall Street Journal*, 30 July 1991, p. 1)

In addition economies of scope offer development and production savings when military and civil products have essential synergies. These benefits of cross-subsidy in the American industry are neatly summarized by Laura Tyson: 'All of the nation's commercial aircraft producers have been major defense contractors, at least at critical moments in their development. The enormous flow of federal government contracts has provided profits (and even in some cases covered tooling costs) that could be applied to the development of commercial aircraft', (Tyson, 1992, p. 169).

The dual-use KC-135/707 program was a clear example of successful defense/commercial synergy. Production of the two aircraft shared the same plant and at least 20% of the parts and tooling. Both aircraft were derived from a common prototype and had concurrent development programs. Regarding the prototype it must be remembered that the 707 was a revolutionary aircraft and that the military-funded project helped Boeing iron out potential technological glitches. In addition common production runs increased the speed with which progress was made down the learning curve and hastened the arrival of economies of scale. The learning curve is critical in aircraft manufacturing as learning elasticity is estimated at .2, i.e. production costs reduce by 20% with a doubling of output.

Regarding the economics of the 707 the simultaneity of the commercial and defense programs significantly reduced the financial risk of the aircraft's launch. To this day many Boeing officials deny the significance of the dual development but in an authoritative study of the Boeing Aircraft Corporation by M. J. Hardy we find the following:

Without the huge KC-135A programme there would almost certainly have been no Model 707, as its unit costs would have been too high, especially without the benefits of using some KC-135 jigs and tooling ... and it was not until 1963, when just over 1000 of the 707, 720, and KC-135/C-135 series had been sold, that Boeing finally passed the break-even point on its jet transport programme, (Hardy, 1982, p. 66).

Table 2.2   **Boeing Aircraft Military Orders 1950-1959**

YEAR	AIRCRAFT TYPE	UNITS
1950	B-47	82
	C-97	14
1951	B-47/RB-47	590
	TB-50	24
	KC-97	231
1952	B-47	788
	B-52	13
	KC-97	231
1953	B-47	864
	B-52	43
	KC-97	262
1954	B-52	25
1955	B-52	77
	KC-135	29
1956	B-52	133
	KC-135	68
1957	B-52	213
	KC-135	118
1958	B-52	101
	KC-135	130
	VC-137	3
	CH-46 Chinook	3
1959	B-52	39
	KC-135	81
	CH-47 Chinook	5

Source: *United States Navy/Air Force Serials*, ed. Peter A. Danby, statistical
analysis, Peter Cullen.

With the backing of Department of Defense (DoD) funding and the strategic
capability to out manoeuvre its US competitors, Boeing emerged in the 1950s as
the dominant force in world aeronautics. As table 2.2 above shows in total Boeing
was contracted to produce 4,422 aircraft by the Pentagon in the 1950s, the period
when the foundations of its future global supremacy in commercial manufacture

were being laid. It is known that 725 of the various commercial versions of the 707 had been produced by 1978, and another 68 were built to serve as Airborne Warning and Control System aircraft (AWACs). But profitability was greatly assisted by the 820 KC-135s that were ordered by the Pentagon before production was closed down in 1966. But the effectiveness of Boeing's strategy based on the Dash 80 cannot and should not be evaluated purely in financial terms. The development of the 707 was a strategic coup as 'Allen's jet program strengthened Boeing's leading military position and put the company firmly in the desirable commercial business while killing off, weakening, or overshadowing all its competitors', (Rodgers, p. 199). In the spring of 1959 Boeing launched the 727 tri-jet; a 120-150 seat short/medium range transport, beginning the creation of a full family of aircraft, which Douglas was never to achieve.

Conclusion

In the 1950s US aeronautical firms, particularly Boeing, by virtue of their participation in large military contracts, developed the technology and expertise necessary to make jet airliners, and they aggressively pursued the opportunities created by their early lead. Although owned and controlled by private capitalists, the US aeronautics firms of the 1950s and 1960s (and the commercial product line they were able to offer to the world, through which they created and then dominated an entire new industry) owed their impressive industrial capabilities and dominant market position to government funding. Boeing had been especially astute in converting the KC-135 tanker into the 707, and then followed upon its success with improved derivatives that provided operators with the cost benefits of owning a common fleet of aircraft. Outmaneuvering both its European and American rivals, by the mid-1960s Boeing had become the dominant firm in a new and rapidly expanding market: 'These advantages enabled Boeing to establish the industry standard of excellence in technology, manufacturing, marketing and product service', (Yoshino, 1986, p. 520). Moreover, at that time the huge US market was controlled regarding pricing and fare structures and therefore, 'the regulated, large domestic market provided a strong base of demand for technological innovation by the aircraft producers, (Tyson, 1992, p. 171). Once established, mainly because of economies of scale that raised further barriers to entry, the market power of American firms in the world civil aviation market continued to grow well into the 1970s. What is remarkable, as we show below, is that this great advantage was ultimately surrendered.

In the 1960s the 747 and 737 followed the 707 and 727, giving Boeing a family of aircraft with which to achieve global market dominance. By the end of the 1960s overall US domination was such that it had 90% of the world's large commercial aircraft orders and was responsible for 82% of the civil jets that had been manufactured up until 1969.

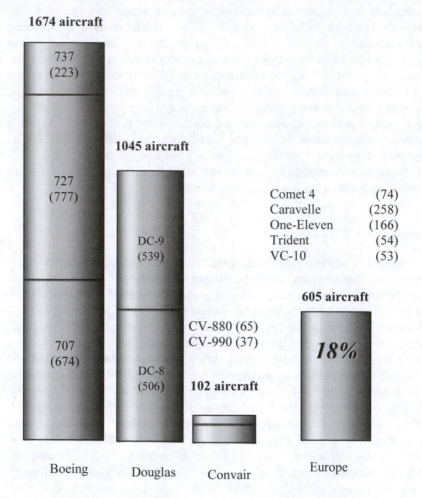

Figure 2.10   Dominance of US Manufacturers in 1969

Chapter 3

Extending the Product Range: From Financial Disaster to Market Dominance

A Product Family

Boeing's success in the 1950s and 1960s came from skillfully applying technologies developed on military projects, such as the B-47, to the business of building commercial jets like the 707 and the 720. In addition to establishing the firm as one of only two American companies at all successful in building commercial jet transports, the success of the 707 and the 720 also demonstrated to Boeing the wisdom of using a family of aircraft as a commercial strategy, in which derivatives and modifications of existing designs were tailored to address market niches and even to fit the needs of specific airlines.

Figure 3.1   **Boeing 720**

The Boeing 727

Not one to rest on his laurels, by 1956 Bill Allen had already tasked Boeing engineers to investigate the development of a jetliner smaller in size and shorter in range than the 707 or 720. Many within the company thought that segment of the market overcrowded with contenders, and board approval in 1959 for the proposed 727 was conditional on getting preliminary orders from at least two major US airlines. Having secured a commitment from United and Eastern to purchase 40 apiece, Allen provided Boeing with an escape clause; if 100 727s had not been sold by 1 December 1960 the program would be scrapped. With United agreeing to take another 20 on option, on 30 November 1960 Allen signed contracts with the two airlines totaling $420m: 'then the largest single transaction in commercial aviation history', (Rodgers, 1996, p. 213).

Figure 3.2   Boeing 727

The first 727 was rolled out on 27 November 1962, and flew for the first time on 9 February 1963. Delivered to Eastern Airlines in October 1963, its first scheduled commercial flight took place in February 1964. Although designed around an innovative wing, with a triple-slot construction that allowed it to be adjusted in size and shape to fill numerous and demanding roles for take-off, cruising and landing, the 727 utilized the fuselage of the 707 to reduce design and productions costs. The 727 was powered by Pratt and Whitney's newest fan jet, the JT8D, arranged around the tail of the aircraft in a three-engine configuration; a concept borrowed directly from the British de Havilland Trident. Despite significant early problems with the engines, the 727 performed better than expected, and sold rapidly. Combined with the success of the 707/720, the 727 program propelled Boeing's commercial fortunes to new milestones, 'In 1964, commercial sales for the first time exceed military and government sales. The next year, Boeing passenger airlines became the most widely used: 36.2 percent of all passenger airlines flying had been made by Boeing, compared with 26.8 percent for Douglas aircraft, (Rodgers, p. 216).

The Boeing 737

With the 727 having firmly established Boeing as the industry leader, Allen prepared to take on the competition both domestic and foreign in the latest emerging market segment. While electing not to challenge the 727 directly, Douglas had designed an even smaller-capacity aircraft having only two jet engines, and was busy taking orders for the new model, designated DC-9. The British had also devised a credible entrant, the BAC One-Eleven, and Boeing seemed in danger of missing a major market opportunity as by early 1965 some 200 DC-9s and 100 BAC One-Elevens had been sold in the US and elsewhere. Allen's response, tentative at first, was the so-called 'baby Boeing', predictably designated the 737. Approved by the Boeing board on 1 February 1965, the German carrier Lufthansa served as Boeing's first foreign launch customer, ordering 21 737s at a price of US$4m each. United Airlines followed with an order for 40 with options on 30 more, and the 737 program was on its way. The aircraft's first flight was 9 April 1967 and was delivered to the two airlines that same December.

With the 737, Boeing again had sought to capitalize on past investments that had been funded in part from military programs, and opted for the same fuselage cross section on the 737 that had been used for the 707 and 727 models. The strategy proved successful in the head-to-head sales battles with Douglas, as the 737 was slightly larger in diameter than the DC-9. Faced so soon after the 707/DC-8 struggle with a second round of intensive competition with a better-funded rival, Douglas sold DC-9s at what proved to be unprofitable prices. By the end of 1966 the once dominant company was forced to merge with the defense contractor McDonnell, forming the McDonnell Douglas Corporation (MDC) on 13 January 1967.

Figure 3.3   Boeing 737-300

But problems for Douglas and the DC-9 did not translate easily or quickly into success for Boeing and the 737. Within Boeing itself, the program competed for financial and engineering resources, and as a result came to market later than promised and even then with several nagging problems. The 737 was further burdened in its competition with the DC-9 and BAC One-Eleven by US union demands that the 737 carry three flight crew instead of two, a disadvantage that was not shed until 1981. Indeed, it would be a full 20 years after its launch that the 737 would meet and then surpass the expectations of its designers by becoming the biggest-selling airliner in history. In the mid-1960s, the 737 seemed to be precisely what the company did not need, as along with the SST and the 747 jumbo-jet programs it appeared to be dragging the company towards financial ruin.

The Boeing 747

Up until the 1960s by far the most ambitious development project in the history of commercial aeronautics was the Boeing 747. Given the immense scale of the resources the company would be required to harness, and these in addition to the burdens of the 737 and SST projects, CEO William Allen hoped to revert to a tried and tested formula and to piggyback again on a contract for a new military transport. As had been done with the Dash 80, he hoped to gain government approval for a project that would serve both the needs of the military and commercial purposes of the company. What he had in mind was a gigantic aircraft to be used for the transport of troops and material that would multiply the power projection capability of the military, which also could be modified to carry passengers and cargo. Planning to make use of a massive new fan jet engine under development by General Electric (GE), 'Boeing submitted an unsolicited preliminary proposal for the company's brainchild that persuaded Pentagon officials to sponsor development of such an airplane, which the Air Force designated the C-5. Boeing then helped the officials write the budget paper submitted to Congress to get the project started', (Rodgers, p. 234).

In May 1964, conceptual studies were requested by the Air Force, a contest which resulted in three firms, Boeing, Lockheed and Douglas, all receiving contracts to undertake the daunting task of preparing final bids. Having submitted what they believed to be a credible and thorough proposal, and having been told as much by the selection board, Boeing officials were deeply shocked on 30 September 1965 to learn that Secretary of Defense Robert McNamara had chosen Lockheed to build the C-5.

Figure 3.4   Boeing 747-300

However, compensation was soon at hand. In April 1966 the Pan American board of directors, led by company president Juan Trippe, placed an order with Boeing for 23 passenger and two freight 747s, an order worth US$531m. With air traffic increasing at more than 10% per annum in the mid-1960s, Juan Trippe was convinced that a huge step change in air transport capacity was needed. Both he and Boeing's John Steiner believed that in a few years' time aircraft with more than 350 seats would be required to meet the future demand, (Heppenheimer, 1995, p. 220). But in fact this projection of demand was very risky, and additionally complicated by the expected arrival of an American supersonic transport (SST). At the time many people in the aircraft business believed that the SST would make subsonic civil jets obsolete. Also no other carriers shared Pan Am's view of the market. Nevertheless, driven forward by the power of its fanatical launch customer, Boeing proceeded to design and build the 747.

After a surprisingly short time a rollout for the first 747 took place in September 1968, with a first flight on 9 February 1969. The aircraft exhibited a surprising ease of handling, but serious problems emerged with the Pratt and Whitney (P&W) JT9D engines, and severe recriminations occurred between Boeing and P&W. in fact Boeing had also been interested in the GE TF-39, an engine that was also being developed in partnership with USAF for the C-5, but the GE engine did not have enough thrust for the 747. P&W, the market leader, came late into the C-5A competition with the JT9D, but the power plant was a huge disappointment to Boeing. Indeed, it can be argued that the JT9D's failings initiated P&W's long-term retreat in the commercial engine market. Boeing executives were furious with the engine supplier and as a result Rolls-Royce was invited to provide engines for the aircraft. To Boeing's great embarrassment when 747s first emerged from the huge doors at Everett there were no engines and the aircraft were, in effect, only gliders, with 9,600 lb concrete blocks slung under their wings.

747 Problems

The fourth 747 was flown to Paris for the airshow in spring 1969. However, there were difficulties with FAA certification, which was not completed until December 1969, so that Pan Am missed the chance to book holiday travelers over the summer season. Pan Am and Boeing disagreed over the failure to progress the project and Pan Am withheld payments, which began to squeeze Boeing financially. But finally the carrier took delivery of the first of the 25 it had ordered in the summer 1970, and even exercised an option for eight more.

But Pan Am had trouble filling its 747s, and Douglas came out with its rival DC-10, with a first flight in August 1970. As we have seen only Pan Am seemed to think that an aircraft as big as the 747 was necessary for the growing market. The DC-10 had two-thirds the capacity of the 747 and was two-thirds of the cost. A similar tri-jet aircraft, the Lockheed L-1011 also flew just three months later.

As both John Newhouse and Laura Tyson have noted, the launch of three wide-bodied jets in the US in the 1970s was a strategic blunder; one which, as we show in Chapter 4, opened up a major opportunity for Airbus' A300. While making serious competition for Boeing and the 747, the two tri-jets split the market and both were financial disasters for the companies (and for Rolls-Royce on the L-1011). Only 446 DC-10s were sold before the program was ended in 1980, while just 244 L-1011s were built before the program terminated in 1981. Arguably, the DC-10 was also undermined commercially by two high-profile fatal accidents in 1974 and 1979, the latter leading to the temporary withdrawal of the aircraft's certificate of airworthiness.

Financial Woes

In 1965 Boeing had produced more aircraft than ever before and the company was flush with cash. But pressures from the very abbreviated development schedule of the 747 contributed to a financial hemorrhage and the near ruin of the company. The cost of the new giant factory, where the 747 was to be built, at the former military base Paine Field in Everett, also dug deep into Boeing's reserves. As the recession that had begun in late 1968 deepened, the projected high rates of air traffic growth that Trippe had foreseen failed to emerge, and orders from airlines began to fall in 1969. Newhouse highlights the original risk:

> Usually, a new airplane reflects the needs of the market; thus, it is a compromise-not an ideal fit for any one of the big airlines but close enough to what they think they need to be generally acceptable. The 747 was not a compromise; the only American carrier that wanted an airplane that large was Pan Am, and it is unlikely that the major foreign airlines wanted it either. But rightly or wrongly – wrongly in retrospect – they all felt they had no alternative. The big foreign carriers were unwilling to concede Pan Am a major marketing advantage, (Newhouse, 1982, p. 123).

Between 1969 and 1972 Boeing received no orders for the 747 from domestic carriers, (Tyson, 1992, p. 186). As well as the failure of the market to conform to expectations, there were also other problems. The huge cost overruns of the 747 required heavy borrowing, Boeing officials spent a lot of time in New York trying to convince a consortium of banks to keep the financial taps open just a while longer. Major suppliers were prevailed upon to defer billing, but by October 1969 the real prospect of bankruptcy loomed over Boeing. In 1970 Bill Allen and his chief financial officer, Hal Haynes, made a last desperate attempt to increase the company's line of credit, but the foray failed, with disastrous consequences for many individuals and households, (Heppenheimer, 1995, p. 239). The Seattle economy, that had now become so dependent on the company's fortunes, was also seriously depressed. Unemployment in the city was the highest in the US and Seattle's Japanese sister city, Kobe, was sending food parcels and relief funds.

The new Boeing president Thornton Wilson ordered drastic cost cutting; salary cuts for executives and waves of layoffs ensued, with 5000 redundancies in one week alone. Wilson himself had a heart attack on 13 January 1970 (on a flight from Seattle to Washington to witness the christening of Pan Am's first 747 by First Lady Pat Nixon), quite probably brought on by the stress. Yet business conditions worsened further during 1970, and unsold planes (known as white tails) accumulating at Renton were parked out of sight behind the hangars, so as not to occasion too much anguish. Over the years Boeing executives have jibed that Airbus produced white tails in the 1970s but this is precisely what happened to Boeing in 1970/1971. Disaster for the workforce was imminent. In 1968 Boeing had had over 100,000 employees at its Seattle plants; by 1971 the number was 37,000, (Newhouse 1982, pp. 169-170).

A billion dollars in debt by early 1971, the company received an additional blow with the Congressional cancellation of the SST on 24 March 1971; 8,000 Boeing employees were laid off in a single day. But Eugene Rodgers notes that the SST cancellation was probably a blessing in disguise, in that Boeing was able to stop paying into the program. But also the government refunded the US$31.6m that had been spent on it so far. 'Since no other company could undertake an SST program, moreover, Boeing got rid of the expensive millstone without losing ground to a competitor', (Rodgers, p. 302).

Boeing sold off buildings and equipment, and even seriously considered selling the entire 737 program to the Japanese. Survival was touch and go. According to Tyson, orders for the 727 and military contracts were the sole reasons for the company's survival, (Tyson, 1992, p. 186). Gradually, the drastic measures introduced by Wilson began to work, and 'A small but steady flow of military and space program orders kept cash flowing in', (Rodgers, p. 317).

Boeing then decided to stimulate commercial sales by offering a new and improved version of the 727-200 using upgraded JT8D engines and thus having increased speed and range, and the market responded. Financial recuperation began in earnest as 'the airlines snapped up the new airplanes as fast as Boeing could build them, and sales soared past Boeing's modest targets', (Rodgers, p. 318). Also helping the recovery was Douglas' decision in 1972 to end production of the DC-8, which perked up lagging 707 sales just enough for the pioneering aircraft to begin paying its own way again. The 707 also bore fruit yet again on the military side, as the Pentagon awarded Boeing a contract in 1970 to convert the venerable plane for use as an Airborne Warning and Control System (AWACS). The company also began to realize real gains in labor productivity as a result of the merciless cost cutting, 'Like fire that hardens metal, the economic conflagration had strengthened Boeing's efficiency to a degree unprecedented in its history', (Rodgers, p. 321).

Success of the 747

The 747 went on to be hugely profitable: 'It has become a cash cow, a product the company milks steadily for high profits' (Rodgers, p. 287). But at the time of the program launch it was a risky decision, made with little real analysis of the market. It also illustrates very well the disproportionate power of launch customers in the civil aircraft business. Without the Pan Am order the 747 could not have been launched and the airline's president, Juan Trippe, played his trump card for all it was worth. The net result was that by following Trippe's vision Boeing nearly bankrupted itself. Incredibly, with development costs of US$1.2 billion, Boeing was spending three times its total capitalization value on the program.

But in retrospect it must be acknowledged that the 747 decision was not just courageous, but also farsighted. By developing an aircraft with three times the passenger capacity of the 707 and much greater range, Boeing achieved a huge productivity breakthrough in aviation. The economic gains in seat/mile cost paved the way for a new rapid spurt of growth auguring in the dawn of the era of mass air transportation. Perhaps the one real irony of the risky 747 decision is that Boeing subsequently became very cautious and reluctant to invest in new product.

To offer a balanced view it should be acknowledged that at the time of the 747 launch some concern with the risk was evident in Juan Trippe's requirements. One of the virtues of the 747 was that it was designed for easy conversion to a cargo aircraft. Both Trippe and Allen were aware that in order to make money the aircraft had to be flexible. Trippe believed that when the aircraft was not carrying passengers it should bear cargo. Before long dedicated freighter and Combi versions were being produced. The aircraft also allowed for significant development, which came with the -300 and -400 series. By 1993 more than 1000 747s has been sold and by the turn of the century half the world's airfreight was being carried by 747 freighters. The aircraft has also been very profitable. With a ticket price on some models of up to US$200m and with no real discounts available the 747 has been a very lucrative monopoly product for Boeing.

The 747-400

In the early 1980s Boeing decided to develop a 747 with an extended upper deck, designated 747-300. The seated area behind the flight deck was 23 feet (7 meters) longer than the earlier version. However, the 747-300 was soon superseded by the 747-400, which began development in 1985. This new 747 was larger, more powerful, and had longer range than its predecessors. It had the -300's extended upper deck and as well as six-foot winglets on each wing tip to reduce drag. The new version could accommodate 416 to 524 passengers.

The 747-400 has also been a success with over 600 units sold. But the development of the 747-400 illustrated some problems which were also very evident at Boeing in the 1990s. As we saw above the recession of the late 1960s led to huge lay-offs at the Boeing Company. Nearly two-thirds of the workforce was fired. At the time of the 747-400's development Boeing was hiring large number of new staff, as there was an upturn in orders. But 'Hire and Fire' is not a good way to run an aircraft business. Aircraft are highly complex products with millions of components and a large number of complex systems. The skills and competencies to design and build aircraft that are needed in the workforce can only be built up slowly. With the 747-400 Boeing found that its new workforce was not up to the job. 'Hire and Fire' was causing big problems.

The new and inexperienced workforce that had been hired after the end of the latest recession found the design of the 747-400 too complex to integrate. Boeing managers ordered compulsory overtime and 60-hour working weeks became commonplace. But the problems also affected other Boeing planes and complaints from customers about operational problems began to mount. In consequence, 'the Federal Aviation Administration (FAA) ordered special inspections of all Boeing jetliners produced since 1980 to look for defects that might affect safety', (US

Centennial of Flight Commission, 2003). The forced overtime also started to adversely affect industrial relations, leading to a 48-day strike in the autumn of 1989, which hurt Boeing financially, (US Centennial of Flight Commission, 2003).

The problems associated with the 747-400 derivative, which took three years to develop, were magnified in 1997/1998 when Boeing suffered a complete industrial meltdown, leading to the sacking of commercial airplanes head Ron Woodard. This 1990s disaster is explored in more detail in Chapter 8.

Interlude: Boeing and the Strange Case of the US Supersonic Transport

Visitors to Seattle may notice that the home basketball team is known as the 'Sonics', short for supersonic. The name goes back to the time when the city believed that Boeing would make a US rival to Concorde, the Anglo-French supersonic airliner. But the US aircraft was cancelled. Boeing also walked away from the High Speed Research project in 1999 after NASA had spent more than US$1.5 billion on the program. But why was the supersonic transport (SST) cancelled?

Origins of the SST

The Federal Aviation Act was signed into law by President Eisenhower on 23 August 1958. The new Federal Aviation Agency (FAA) was given 'sole responsibility for the control of US airspace and the development of a common civil-military system of air traffic control', (Kent, 1980, p. iii). The second head of the FAA, Najeeb 'Jeeb' Halaby, appointed by President Kennedy in 1961, was pivotal in the US thinking about an SST. This is interesting in itself, as US commentators tend to deny that the US has anything approaching an industrial policy for aerospace. But with the SST high politics and aircraft development walked hand in hand.

The most controversial of the projects undertaken by Najeeb Halaby during his tenure at the FAA concerned the possible development of a SST in the United States, with the federal government and the FAA playing a major role in the project. As the US military began to redirect its research and development efforts from winged aircraft to ballistic missiles, Halaby shared the concerns of many in the industry for the future of American leadership in commercial aeronautics, (Kent, 1980, p. 42). Richard Kent outlines the problem Halaby had identified:

> The American aircraft industry had reached an important crossroads at the beginning of the 1960s. The United States had become the world leader in developing and producing civil aircraft, largely as a result of heavy military investment in aviation since World War II. Aeronautical technology produced by this military investment had been easily transferred to civil aviation. But just as the time arrived for the development of the next generation of aircraft, which would consist of a fleet of air transports capable of

supersonic flight, the military had shifted the major part of its research efforts to ballistic missiles. Without this traditional means of support, American aircraft manufacturers faced an uncertain future, (Kent, 1980, p. 42).

Given his anxiety about the industry Halaby successfully sought an appropriation of US$12m from the federal purse. This was included in Kennedy's supplemental 1962 budget for the FAA to initiate a feasibility study of a commercial SST. But seeing his project narrowly survive a Congressional challenge and its funding cut to US$11m, Halaby acted decisively to create a Supersonic Transport Management Office within the FAA, whose efforts would be coordinated with representatives from NASA and the Department of Defense, through a Supersonic Transport Steering Group. To further mollify critics of these expensive initiatives, Halaby compelled industry to contribute to the SST development efforts: 'He insisted upon a cost-sharing provision in the contracts to impress all that the Kennedy administration did not consider the development of an SST a Federal giveaway program', (Kent, p. 45). But while the manufacturers were pleased to participate in a cohesive government-industry partnership on such a commercially risky project, the airlines were less than enthusiastic about attempts to develop a technology that, if successful, might render obsolete their recent and heavy investments in conventional jets. Halaby therefore had to promise the potential customers for the SST 'a major voice in the design characteristics of the American effort in return for their support', (Kent, p. 43).

International Rivalry

Throughout 1962, Halaby found himself the focal point of a debate on the technical and commercial feasibility of an American SST, and his advocacy for accelerating the program ran into formidable opposition within the Kennedy Administration and on Capitol Hill. Not to be pushed too quickly, President Kennedy appointed a special Cabinet committee chaired by Vice-President Johnson, which evaluated Halaby's revised cost estimates and passed on to the President a positive recommendation on the SST on the 30 May 1963. Despite the deliberate pace of the Kennedy administration's decision that the government should fund and organize the American efforts to develop the next generation of commercial aircraft, it is clear that the pressures of 'international rivalry played an important role in race to the SST', (Kent, p. 102). Kent also notes that: 'In a period when French President Charles de Gaulle was challenging the United States' hegemony of Western Europe, nothing could have pleased President Kennedy better than a head-to-head rivalry on the SST', (p. 102).

Not only had the British and French governments joined forces to support the efforts of their respective national firms to develop the Concorde, but the pre-eminent US airline, Pan Am, had agreed to purchase six of the new aircraft, (Kent, p. 103). Europe was threatening to steal the lead position from the US in a high technology sector. However, in this case the US government's priorities were not the same as those of the American airframe manufacturers and engine builders, which objected to the proposal that they commit themselves to contribute approximately 20% of the development costs for the SST.

Anxious that the project not be derailed by such details, Halaby pressed forward by releasing on 15 August 1963 the FAA's formal 'Request for Proposals for the Development of a Commercial Supersonic Transport', while redoubling his efforts to convince Congress, the manufacturers and the airlines of the project's viability. Halaby prevailed upon President Kennedy to create a committee of prominent figures from the financial community to draw up recommendations on how an American SST might be designed, produced and operated in a manner consistent with the interests of all concerned in industry and government. Kennedy chose for the job a former president of the World Bank, Eugene Black, and the Chairman of the Board of Olin Mathieson, Stanley de J. Osbourne. Faced with the real prospect of additional US airlines ordering the European version of the SST, Halaby attempted to use his position as FAA Administrator 'to get American carriers to place advance orders for the American aircraft', (Kent, p. 104).

By late 1963, Najeeb Halaby had therefore left no stone unturned in his effort to employ the political leverage of his office to make an American SST a technological and commercial reality.

Despite the turmoil surrounding the succession of Lyndon Johnson to the presidency following the assassination of President Kennedy in November 1963, the SST program remained of central concern to the new administration. Having received the Black and Osborne report on 19 December 1963, Johnson continued to employ the talents of its authors through their participation on the President's Advisory Committee on Supersonic Transport (PAC). Although Najeeb Halaby was also a PAC member, he found his former influence on the form and pace of the SST program much diluted. Taking seriously the findings of the Black and Osborne report, in May 1964 the PAC and its chairman, Secretary of Defense McNamara, extended the SST design competition for six months, and then for another six months, quite evidently seeing scant political virtue in rushing the sensitive selection process. Of even greater concern to Halaby was the report's questioning of his and the FAA's proper role and responsibilities relative to the SST project, raising as it did the specter of a conflict of interest. But there as an obvious question: how could the FAA develop an aircraft it would then certificate: 'Even if the agency could handle the management problems, a serious conflict of interest would exist in the agency's responsibility to certificate an aircraft that it was itself developing. FAA might also have difficulty remaining neutral in certificating the competing Concorde', (Kent, p. 106).

Halaby's Departure

As it turned out, these were battles Halaby was not to fight, as he was replaced in the summer of 1965, well before the SST program had moved beyond the design competition phase. The competitive pressures felt so strongly by Halaby to move quickly on an American SST had been relieved substantially by the decision that Spring of the British government to cancel the BAC TSR2 tactical strike/reconnaissance aircraft, whose performance characteristics were expected to provide the Concorde project managers with a great deal of useful information on the Olympus engine chosen to power the European aircraft. In effect the UK took the political and technological pressure off the US by backing off from the TSR2.

Under these new circumstances, Halaby could agree to support the PAC recommendation of May 1965 that the American SST program be given an additional 18 months to test demonstrator engines and refine the airframe design. It would be left to his successor to sort out the proper role for the FAA in both developing and regulating the commercial use of an as yet untested technology.

Although his appointment and confirmation were the occasion of considerable controversy, retired four-star USAF General William F. McKee assumed the top position at the FAA in July 1965, willing and able to play an active part in formulating the nation's commercial aviation policy, especially relative to the SST, (Kent, p. 144). Not only was the program running dangerously short of funds even as the design competition between Boeing and Lockheed was intensifying, the FAA was also involved in the complex process of determining the characteristics and implications of the sonic boom associated with SST technology. Tests conducted at Edwards Air Force base during 1966 revealed that 'sonic boom would preclude the flight of all SSTs, including the Concorde, on overland routes', (Kent, p. 144). Clearly, such restrictions would appear to seriously compromise the commercial viability of the technology, as 'SSTs would be limited to the relatively few overseas routes, where they would face stiff competition from the new generation of jumbo jets scheduled to enter service at the end of the decade', (Kent, p. 144).

However, after evaluating the potential damage that might be done to the US aircraft manufacturing industry if leadership in SST technology was conceded to the Europeans, and considering the further erosion in the balance of trade that would be caused by the purchase of European aircraft by US airlines, the PAC decided on 22 December 1966 to accept the most recent FAA findings and recommend to President Johnson that Phase III of the SST project should begin. It envisioned a four-year program of prototype development, and General McKee had the privilege of announcing that the team of Boeing and General Electric (GE) had won the competition to build it, (Kent, p. 296).

The Technical Challenges

Despite the surge of optimism concerning the prospects for an American SST, Boeing began to immediately experience serious problems with its design, in particular the variable configuration wing: 'The integrity of Boeing's innovative variable wing design had not been fully established when it was submitted for review to FAA engineers in late 1966 ... Design changes invariably added weight that altered both the economics of the aircraft (reduced its effective payload) and its ability to operate out of existing airports' (Kent, p. 296)

Although working closely with FAA engineers throughout 1967 to correct these defects, Boeing was unable to meet the criteria established for the requirements review of 15 January 1968, and proposed the consideration of alternative designs. Reluctantly the FAA agreed, but imposed rigorous new terms, requiring that Boeing come up with a viable design by 15 January 1969 or liable for government funds spent and any cost overruns experienced by GE because of the redesign. Responding effectively to these pressures, Boeing produced a more conservative prototype configuration based on a fixed wing and having somewhat less seating capacity than originally projected but yet remaining, at least according to the FAA, an economically viable aircraft.

Unfortunately for the SST program's supporters, the FAA evaluation of Boeing's redesign that began in December 1968 corresponded precisely with the presidential transition and the incoming Nixon administration was determined to launch its own review of the controversial project, raising the possibility of further delays, (Kent, p. 298). But despite concerns raised in the review about the aircraft's noise levels and some possible environmental effects, President Nixon finally agreed to accept the recommendation of his Transportation Secretary, Volpe, and on 23 September 1969 Nixon announced his intention to press forward with the program. A budget request of US$96m was approved by Congress and, as '1969 ended, the American SST program appeared to have passed one of its last political obstacles', (Kent, p. 301).

The Environmental Lobby: the End of the SST

Even as the SST began to clear technological, economic and financial hurdles, during 1969 nagging concerns surrounding its potential environmental impact were being transformed into opposition potent enough to eventually kill the program. What had begun as expressions of shock at the damage to beaches and marine life caused by the blowout of an oil well off the California coast in the Santa Barbara Channel on 28 January 1969, was transformed into a protest movement of extreme social and political significance: environmentalism.

American environmentalism chimed with other radical 1960s movements, which were both anti-establishment and anti-technology. Indeed, leading US sociologist Peter Berger spoke of this period as the 'greening of America'. This newest form of 1960s social and political activism gave the project's opponents of the SST a new lease on life, and even some within the Nixon administration expressed serious environmental reservations about proceeding with the SST program. In Congress during 1970 Senator William Proxmire brought witnesses before the Joint Subcommittee on Economy in Government to testify to the extreme noise levels that would be associated with the SST (especially during takeoff), and to raise concerns about possible damage to the earth's stratosphere from the aircraft's exhaust. One witness, the IBM physicist Richard Garwin, asserted that the SST would make as much noise at take-off as 50 jumbo jets, (Heppenheimer, 1995, p. 244).

As well as his environmental concerns Proxmire attacked the proposed funding for the SST. The plan involved the FAA putting up US$1.3 billion for development and production of two prototypes. Thereafter Boeing would repay the funds on a royalty basis. Proxmire said it was a subsidy, but the project head, William Magruder, argued that it was a loan. As he remarked, 'By the time the 300th airplane is sold, all of the governments money will be returned to the treasury, and when we sell 500 airplanes, there will be a billion dollars in profit to the Government', (Quoted, Heppenheimer, p. 244). Magruder's comments are interesting because what he outlined is precisely the funding mechanism that European governments have used for Airbus programs; a mechanism Boeing have always claimed was illegitimate.

In Congress, Proxmire's arguments were to prove decisive. Following an unexpectedly narrow House of Representatives vote of support for continued appropriations for fiscal year 1971, opponents and supporters brought all of their resources to bear on the debate in the Senate: 'When the December 3 [1970] vote was tallied, the Senate had voted to reject the administration's 1971 SST appropriation request', (Kent, p. 305).

Although the project staggered on into the early weeks of the New Year, by the end of March 1971 both houses of Congress had voted the program down, and the American version of the supersonic transport aircraft was officially deceased. Kent puts it thus; 'The SST would be the symbolic sacrificial lamb killed on the altar of the environment', (p. 301).

But, of course, this defeat for the American SST also had severe consequences in Europe. The decision not to build a US supersonic was based on an argument that also destroyed the commercial prospects for Concorde. But in Europe Concorde's fate was construed in two very contrasting ways. The British lamented it as a white elephant based on a bogus business case while the French construed it as a technology demonstrator for Airbus.

Conclusion: Getting Boeing Back on Track

In many ways the SST was a diversion for Boeing when it was struggling with the 747. The technical failures and problems on the SST at the company are well characterized by Boeing designer Edward Wells:

> The strange thing about the … SST experience was that the more we came to know, the less-well things worked out for us. Instead of entering a situation where the problems began to offset one another, the problems were actually compounding. Where they should have started to converge, they continued to diverge. They were beginning to point more and more in the same direction, to a conclusion that we had been trying to hold off, (Quoted Heppemheimer, 1995, p. 241).

All in all, 1971 looked like a disastrous year for Boeing: a number of 747s remained unsold, 50,000 workers were laid off and now the 2707 SST had been cancelled. But Boeing was not the only US aerospace giant in deep trouble. Lockheed was also facing bankruptcy and was only rescued by a federal loan guarantee of US$250m.

However, in responding to the crisis of the late 1960s Boeing made changes that served it well in the future. Despite the problems of the 747 and the cancellation of the SST, Boeing had the 737, 727 and the 707. The company began to rationalize production by consolidating all three programs at Renton and radically changing working practices. Better control of inventory and availability of components meant that workers were spending longer on the line and less time wondering off in search of parts and equipment, (Heppenheimer, p. 255). As a result the lead-time from order to delivery on the 727 and 737 was reduced from 17 to 11 months by 1972.

Overall, by the early 1970s, the US had more than 90% of the world market for large commercial jets and increasingly that market share belonged to Boeing because of the failings of Douglas and Lockheed. But in Europe the seeds of a response were being sown. The individual states of Europe lacked the resources and large national markets necessary for success in this industry, where scale and scope economies were critical. A new industrial strategy of pan-European collaboration was required and, as if to prove that necessity is indeed the mother of invention, in the late 1960s the grounds were being laid to create Airbus Industrie. The riposte to *La Défi Americain* was under way.

Chapter 4

European Renaissance: The Rise of Airbus

Introduction

Given the near total American control of the world civil airframe market illustrated in Chapter 2, the aeronautics firms and national governments of the major European states had to engage in a calculated gamble if they were to revive their industry. In order to save and then regenerate their capability in the production of commercial airliners, and thus regain the right to engage the Americans in a battle for current and future market share in a high-cost, high-risk, oligopolistic industry, the Europeans had to devise and implement a strategy capable of changing the very rules of the game. Those who had been fierce competitors would now have to co-operate in order to challenge, equal and then surpass their American rival.

The stakes in the new battle with the US were high. In the 1960s certain European leaders and a handful of industrialists realized that the battle for control of civil aeronautics was part of a bigger game. From their vantage point the design, production and marketing of aircraft constituted the operational level of a larger strategic contest, therefore making the aircraft themselves the point of contact in an economic and industrial rivalry of much broader scope. At stake were more than the benefits of high value-added employment or technological spin-offs, or even the prestige of building aircraft. Due to its strategic character and embodiment of high technology, the aircraft industry symbolized the technological and political potency of the nation in world affairs. The European business and political leaders who forged Airbus did not want to succumb to total technological dependence on America. To be knocked out of the aircraft business by the US would therefore have constituted a huge loss in terms of reputation and strategic capability.

The Creation and Development of Airbus Industrie

The fruit of this strategic thinking and also the most important development in commercial aeronautics during this period was the re-emergence of a European capability in large airframe manufacturing in the form of Airbus Industrie, a consortium of national firms supported by their respective governments. In order to be successful, not only would the Europeans have to accommodate the distinctive interests and capabilities of the respective national firms and governments, they also would have to do so in a way that translated commercial imperatives into a business strategy capable of first regaining a foothold in the global market for commercial airliners, and then wresting the technological and industrial initiative from the Americans.

The products of the largest American manufacturers (McDonnell Douglas and especially Boeing) were the concrete representation of US leadership in the aeronautics industry and also of overall American political and economic dominance in the Cold War era. The characteristics of the American commercial aircraft product (range, payload, reliability and fuel consumption) defined the very terms in which any prospective European response to the American challenge would have to be expressed. In order to be effective, European political and economic aspirations would have to be translated into the same currency as used by the Americans: a line of aircraft with performance characteristics comparable to existing products, yet able to attract demand in a market in which the terms of competition had already been set by the leading firms. The challenge was awesome as the incumbent firms had the benefits of hugely expensive capital equipment, partly funded by government, and economies of scale and scope from the existing size and variety of their operations. In addition Airbus would have to counter the strong prejudice existing in the US market against any non-American producer. As Vicki Golich noted, 'US airlines were likely to consider foreign aircraft only if no domestically built alternative existed', (Golich, 1992, p. 918).

The Airbus Players

Prior to the formation of Airbus, individual European countries had tried to co-operate with US partners on a bilateral basis. Boeing expressed an interest in partnering on the de Havilland Trident, while Douglas had similar thoughts regarding the Sud Est Caravelle. But the US companies were not serious about industrial collaboration. In a seminal study of aerospace co-operation Golich writes, 'the 1950s and 1960s were marked by several attempts at co-operation, all of which were aborted unilaterally by the Americans', (Golich, 1992, p. 915). Thus, the radical answer and also the only rational response to US dominance was for Europe's major aerospace nations themselves to collaborate in partnership.

After the mixed experience of the Concorde supersonic program, this move to collaboration bore fruit with the birth of Airbus Industrie in 1970. But the usual European national tensions and differences were not easily put aside and the rise of Airbus was not without its mishaps and conflicts. At the start of the Airbus initiative the British had negotiated a 37.5% work share but the Wilson government pulled out of the project to build the A300, leaving British participation to Hawker Siddeley Aviation (HSA), which committed US$30m towards the development of the A300 wing, (Thornton, 1995, p. 80.) Fortunately for the British company, which was at that time the largest aircraft company in Europe, the German government was keen to employ Britain's wing expertise and agreed to extend financial assistance to HSA so that the project to produce the

A300 (now known as the A300B) moved towards completion in the early 1970s, with a roll out ceremony in Toulouse in September 1972.

UK Ambivalence

It is worth pausing to consider Britain's lukewarm response to Airbus. Not only were the Continental Europeans inconvenienced by the UK government's ambivalence towards the project, they were also frustrated by Rolls-Royce's attempt to provide engines simultaneously for the Lockheed L-1011 as well as the A300. Having originally insisted on a 75% share of the Airbus' RB207 engine, work at the Rolls-Royce Derby plant soon prioritized the US-destined RB211 engine. In essence the British government and Rolls-Royce appeared to be attempting to ensure that Airbus was stillborn. In the US the federal government was fully supportive of its aerospace companies. But in Europe strategy was fragmented, as Britain continued its traditional game of facing simultaneously across the Channel and the Atlantic. Compared to France, where the political elite had a coherent and integrated framework for industrial policy and a matching foreign policy, Britain had neither. Airbus did emerge and prosper, but in the early days this was despite rather than because of any British government contribution. Not surprisingly, dominance on the first Airbus project went to the French, ' ... consistent French support for and commitment to a truly European response to the American challenge in civil aerospace was translated into project leadership on the A300B', (Thornton, 1995, p. 80)). As a result Toulouse became the emotional as well as the physical home of the European aircraft industry.

In the intervening years British commentators have complained that on the Concorde program the UK gave away too much technology to France. But Concorde was the technological precursor to Airbus in which the UK was offered a 37.5% share. It was Britain that failed to capitalize on the Concorde program through its vacillation over Airbus.

Modifying the A300

As we have seen, the initial plan to create the first Airbus was beset by inter-governmental disputes, with the British government and Rolls-Royce pulling out. In addition to these problems there were wider issues regarding the design and specification for the aircraft. Some of the senior players in the new project began to realize that the A300 was not feasible as currently envisaged; the design was too dependent on appeasing diverse political stakeholders. They were also aware that in order to resolve some of the doubts of potential customers, the proposed aircraft had to be commercially viable. The real challenge, therefore, was to retain the political interest, financial support and industrial expertise of all three partners without allowing the aircraft project itself to be held hostage to differences among them.

In mid-1968 Airbus founders Henri Ziegler, Roger Beteille and Felix Kracht took the initiative and secretly redesigned the aircraft. What emerged was the A300B, a smaller 250-seat aircraft now to be powered by General Electric CF6 or Pratt & Whitney JT9D. This was the catalyst for the British government, already cool about the project and anxious about Concorde, to pull out despite the fact that the redesigned aircraft was clearly a more viable commercial proposition. However, HSA kept Britain in the project with strong backing from the West German government. This, of course, was not altruism on the part of West Germany, as Airbus needed British expertise in wing design.

Defying the Critics

At the time of its creation there were many sceptics about Airbus. In 1968 when Beteille and Kracht forced through the A300 redesign there were as yet no firm orders. However, on the back of orders from state-owned Air France, Lufthansa and (later) Iberia the project went ahead. Three years and five months after the agreement to build the A300B, the aircraft took to the skies over Toulouse. What must have surprised the sceptics was that not only had the aircraft met its technical specifications, it had also been produced on time and to cost. Beteille and Kracht had painstakingly instilled a commercial orientation in the Airbus partners, which bore fruit with the A300B. Flight-testing of the aircraft went smoothly and European and American certification was secured in 1974. The first scheduled A300B service began on 23 May 1974 between Paris and London.

The A300B came onto the market at an inauspicious time. In 1973 the fallout from the Yom Kippur War included OPEC's quadrupling of the price of oil. Airlines were in the doldrums as fuel prices skyrocketed and demand for air travel tailed off. But in this context the A300B had some compellingly attractive features. Although the A300B was not in the main a technologically innovative product, in conceptual terms it was radical and it suited a requirement American Airlines had specified for a medium capacity aircraft for short to medium routes.

The Airbus A300, and thus European hopes to re-establish themselves in the commercial airframe business, both benefited and suffered from the fact that the aircraft was introduced at a time of transition and even upheaval in the market. Entering service during the first OPEC oil shock of 1973-74, the fuel-efficient Airbus was attractive to customers, especially in a rapidly internationalizing market with route characteristics matching those for which the A300 was designed. By designing and producing a twin-engine, wide-body, medium-haul plane using American engines and other standard components, the management of Airbus Industrie opted for a tactical move that was cautious yet innovative. Just as the A300 was trying to establish itself, Douglas and Lockheed had begun a disastrous competition for the same market segment with their nearly identical wide-bodied tri-jets. With the addition of the Boeing 747 this meant that three new US wide-body designs were competing in the early 1970s. John Newhouse highlights the opportunity this created, 'the consequence of these [launch] decisions ... injured each of the three suppliers but left in their wake an opportunity for European counties to become something they had never been - a competitive threat to the Americans', (Newhouse, 1982, p. 123). As Newhouse implies, when the market did pick up in 1975, Airbus was potentially better placed with its smaller A300B to meet the airlines more realistic assessment of their requirements. The A300B designers had paid close attention to American Airlines original specification for a new wide-bodied transport. In 1975 33 A300Bs were sold, with another 22 options, more than the DC-10 and L-1011 combined, (Hayward, 1989, pp. 53-55). Airbus was established as a serious competitor to the giant US manufacturers.

Figure 4.1   Airbus A300B

Establishing Airbus's Credibility

The 55 sales and options Airbus achieved in 1975 helped to alleviate the rather gloomy atmosphere in Toulouse but they were not enough to give Airbus real credibility. For Airbus it was clear that establishing credibility in the US was vital. In 1977 an office was opened in New York and George Warde, a former American Airlines President, was hired to run the US operation, (Lynn, 1995, p. 119). Warde's credentials and contacts soon paid dividends. Shortly after he took the Airbus job, Warde presented a sales proposal to Eastern Airlines. Eastern liked the A300 but not enough to buy it there and then. In a deal dubbed 'fly before you buy,' Eastern borrowed a number of A300s to trial on its busy and demanding Miami to New York and Miami to Montreal routes. The aircraft performed extremely well, with high despatch reliability and even better fuel consumption than in the Airbus specification. As a result Eastern Airlines agreed a deal for 23 A300s and a further 25 of the projected new model A310.

At the end of the 1970s there was another oil price rise, which amplified again the advantages of the more economic wide-bodied twin concept. In 1979 Airbus took 132 orders and 89 options. To many peoples' astonishment, after only nine years in the business Airbus was outselling Boeing in the wide-body market. Boeing soon responded with the 767 and 757 but in the context of the 1979 oil crisis it was Airbus who had the right product on the market. Despite the Concorde debacle, the European Industry had been saved. But, in addition, the ground was laid for a bitter and enduring row with the Americans about aircraft trade and subsidy issues. More competition was the last thing US companies wanted, (Lynn, p. 122).

The Airbus GIE

The A300B and its specific range and payload configuration can be viewed as an initial and successful move in a larger strategy but the mechanism of cooperation chosen by the European partners was also crucial in the eventual success of the Airbus venture. Formed under French law as a *Groupement d'Interet Economique* (GIE) rather than as a corporation, the 'GIE format ... was vital in building confidence and credibility amongst airline customers' (Hayward, 1987, p. 19). Particularly important here was the joint and several liability of the industrial partners, with government backing (and even outright state ownership in the case of Aérospatiale) providing the ultimate security to prospective customers. 'In other words, Airbus products had the guarantee of the two powerful European nations – France and Germany – not an insignificant factor in establishing its much needed credibility' (Yoshino, p. 522). The creation of an innovative framework of collaboration among its leading aeronautics firms therefore reinforced the European strategy based on a technically and commercially feasible product. These developments dovetailed nicely with the consortium's overall view of the market and how Airbus might fit into its growth: 'From the beginning, the management of Airbus recognized the need to be a global player if it was to succeed at all', (Yoshino, p. 523).

Despite the daunting challenge of competing with the US incumbents, the Airbus consortium's management was not deterred in its intention to establish the requisite capability to remain in the business over the long haul. Everyone in the commercial airline business recognized that Boeing had attained its commanding position by designing and building a whole family of aircraft, a concept that offered substantial benefits to both customer and manufacturer. As a prospective competitor to the market leader in an oligopolistic industry, Airbus realized that it would have to adopt similar tactics or ultimately fail in its attempt to alter the competitive balance. While the A300 clearly did exploit an existing market gap, alone it could do little to diminish the relative strength of the American producers. The Airbus consortium either had to press onward or else become a one-shot cooperative project having no real impact on the larger strategic situation in the commercial airframe market.

Expanding the Product Line

In the mid-1970s the partners and governments of the Airbus consortium faced a crucial decision concerning how precisely to expand the product family. The French and British partners argued for launching a product addressed to the single-aisle segment of the market and wanted to build an entirely new aircraft to replace the aging 727s and DC-8s of the world airline fleet. However, the Germans pressed hard for '... putting the accent on further establishing the place of Airbus in its original niche ...', (Muller, 1989, p. 179). They sought to build another twin-aisle, twin-engine aircraft. The German position prevailed. But once the fundamental decision to launch a derivative aircraft was taken, the question became whether to shrink the A300 with minor modifications to the basic aircraft or to take a more substantial technological leap.

Airbus's decision to undertake significant new financial and technological risks concerning the configuration and capabilities of the A310 was not merely a response to existing market imperatives. While opting for a substantially modified version of the A300, the consortium hoped to use technological initiative to effect a change in the strategic dynamics of the industry. With the A310, 'the GIE tried to regain control of the market not by launching a completely new product, but in perfecting an existing product so as to make a 'half-generation advance', (Muller, p. 181). Therefore, the decision to build a substantially modified aircraft, even while the consortium's first product still was far from commercially remunerative for the partners or the governments, was a second tactical move primarily based not only on an assessment of short-term financial considerations or existing market opportunities, but also on the place of the new aircraft for the consortium's longer-run strategy: 'With the A310, the European consortium tried to impose upon the market its own specific rhythm of technological change in such a way as to constrain the competition ... ', (Muller, p. 180).

At this point revenue from sales of the A300 had not provided enough capital to finance the necessary investments in technology, tooling and training for investment in a whole product line. Therefore at this juncture we can see most clearly the crucial role played by the political and financial support of the national governments in the ultimate success of the European renaissance in civil aeronautics. The public/private partnership that was established between Airbus and the partner governments created the basis for the consortium's future ability to remain in the business. Partnership with government countered the effects of US industry support and allowed Airbus to overcome the market uncertainties of high costs and long product development lead times. Airbus feels no shame about this, for it was the only way to compete effectively. After all, the US firms were cushioned through to the point of profitability on the civil side by lucrative defense deals and free technology. Laura Tyson notes the scale of the challenge that Airbus faced:

> Given the industry's economics, Airbus would not have stood a chance against American producers without massive development, production and marketing support during the last 25 years. Because of scale, scope and learning economies, a potential entrant to the industry faces much higher production costs than do incumbent firms. It takes years of losses for a new firm to develop a family of aircraft and to produce them on a large enough scale to realize the economies comparable to those enjoyed by existing firms', (Tyson. 1992, p. 157).

Looking at the A300/A310 product line as a two-stage opening gambit, the public/private partnership approach allowed the first line of aircraft to remain in production despite the dearth of sales, and also, because of its long-range approach, allowed the consortium's managers to begin implementation of the next phase of the strategic game plan.

Figure 4.2   Airbus A310

For the US civil airframe manufacturers, Airbus's persistence in building, marketing and designing new aircraft came as an unpleasant and untimely surprise. At first it had seemed safe ignoring the upstart: 'Until the late 1970s, the US manufacturers had dismissed Airbus as just another feeble and disappointing effort of the European commercial aerospace industry', (Yoshino, p. 523). But with the sale to Eastern Airlines in 1978, attitudes in the US industrial and political circles changed rapidly, as Americans recognized that the consortium was 'committed to a fundamental goal that was different from their own', (Yoshino, p. 525). From this point forward, both US aerospace executives and government officials began to perceive the Airbus consortium for what it really was: a means to achieving larger ends in a strategy calculated to reestablish a permanent European competitor in global civil airframe manufacturing and to secure the attendant benefits in jobs, exports and high technology.

New Technology

In order to make good its competitive challenge the European consortium recognized that Airbus would need a key and decisive competitive edge. Airbus sought this in technology. From the A310 onwards Airbus has led the world in technological innovation and dynamic efficiency. With a completely new wing the A310 was not a cheap option for Airbus. But the new wing confirmed Britain's position as the clear world leader in Large Commercial Aircraft (LCA) wing design and coincided with the return of the UK as a full Airbus partner and the creation of the national champion, British Aerospace. The A310 also saw the new and radical Forward Facing Crew Cockpit flight deck (FFCC) based on new computing and avionics. Further, the aircraft introduced wing tip fences and a rear fuel tank placed in the horizontal stabiliser, the latter allowing reconfiguration of the plane's centre of gravity to improve drag and trim characteristics. At the time some scepticism was expressed in Seattle and Long Beach concerning this innovation, but quickly it emerged as an industry standard. The A310 made good Airbus's boast that its aircraft would set the standard for technological advance.

In a 'zero-sum' contest such as the emerging transatlantic struggle in civil airframe manufacturing, success for one player in garnering outside resources also would deny their use to the other. In the late 1970s, therefore, British financial capital and technology represented an important prize for both the Airbus partners and the American manufacturers. Seen from the perspective of strategic engagement, British Aerospace's decision to join Airbus from 1 January 1979, even paying an entry fee for the privilege, was a major victory for the consortium. Although Rolls-Royce and British Airways remained unreconciled to the collaborative effort, once again the national governments of the three major European aeronautics powers were officially committed to the Airbus program. This commitment would prove important not only financially and industrially, especially for the new A310 program, but also in international marketing efforts in regions where British political influence remained strong.

By solidifying the financial, commercial and political prospects of the collective European effort, the official British return to the Airbus program also allowed the consortium to consider more daring options regarding its next move. In relation to the consortium's long-term objectives, the early 1980s were especially important. The market leader, Boeing, had just introduced two new products, the single-aisle 757 and the wide-bodied, twin-engine 767, with the latter a direct competitor of the A300/A310. At this point, the Germans argued for designing a long-range, large-capacity aircraft that would challenge Boeing in that segment of the market in which, with the famed 747, it possessed an outright monopoly. As before, and this time with success, the French pressed for the single-aisle option; in hopes of garnering a significant share of the anticipated 727/DC-9 replacement business, thus opening a completely new market niche for Airbus products. In the end the French view prevailed and Airbus embarked on the A320 program, thus challenging the proposed McDonnell-Douglas MD 80 series and the new 300 and 400 series variants of the Boeing 737.

The Airbus A320

The launch of the single-aisle A320 involved not just the penetration of a new market segment, but also a great technological leap. By introducing a fully computerized flight control system and redesigning the cockpit around new CRT technology, Airbus sought to take a major step in differentiating its products from those proposed by its competitors. Airbus introduced fly-by-wire on the A320, not in the analogue form used on Concorde, but in a digital form linked to new levels of automation in the aircraft's flight management system (FMS). Fly-by-wire meant that the pilot's inputs to control the aircraft's moving surfaces were electronic, rather than directly hydro-mechanical. The traditional yoke was replaced by a side-stick allowing more space in the cockpit. These changes, plus the use of more composite materials, meant significant weight savings; all adding up to significant operational savings for the customer.

Although a single aisle aircraft the A320 had a 3.95m wide cabin offering passengers more room than the US competition. But such an advance would have implications beyond the merely technological: 'With this airplane … [Airbus Industrie] attempted, in making a generational advance, to impose upon the market its own rhythm of generational change, and to establish in its turn the market standard, which would confer upon it leadership in that segment', (Muller, 1989, p. 183). The US government and US manufacturers were clearly shocked. As Laura Tyson notes, 'It was one thing to watch smaller American producers lose market share as a result of a wise European decision on the size and range of the A300, it was quite another to watch Airbus challenge Boeing with a new technology', (Tyson, 1992, pp. 202-203).

Figure 4.3   Airbus A320

The wisdom of the European move was vindicated as the order book for the new aircraft grew rapidly, including major purchases from important airlines in the United States, such as United and Northwest Airlines. To the astonishment of some the A320 became the fastest selling jetliner in history. With the A320, Airbus confronted the American manufacturers, not only with competition in an additional market segment, but also with a product that set new industry standards. This wresting of the technological initiative from the industry's dominant players was thus a very significant element in the consortium's overall strategy. After it introduced the A320, Airbus was no longer merely responding to conditions established by its competitors; now it was influencing directly the very rules under which the competition would take place. Europe was seeking to outgun America in a high technology sector.

The public funding for Airbus was, of course, a counterpoint to the huge government funding provided in the USA. The US companies had large defense orders to counter the effects of the civil business cycle and also received cash overheads on their defense contracts. Moreover, as we saw in Chapter 2, much of the civil technology was derived from military projects where the research and development was paid for from the public purse. On the SST, where risk was perceived to be high, Boeing sought exactly the same kind of funding arrangement with government that was used in Europe, (see Chapter 3).

Footnote: the Other US Competitors

As we noted in Chapter 3, Lockheed and McDonnell-Douglas both made valiant efforts to capture a segment of the wide-body, medium to long-range market with their L-1011 and DC-10 tri-jets. However, as Laura Tyson explains, the launching of near-identical tri-jets turned out to be a disaster for both companies, (Tyson, 1992, p. 186). Interestingly, when one considers the 1960s requirement for a wide-body, originally stipulated by American Airlines, it was Airbus which followed the prompt of the US carrier with its twin-engine concept, while Boeing leapfrogged to the four-engine 747. Clearly there was no space in the middle for two tri-jets; both projects were doomed to commercial failure.

Figure 4.4   McDonnell Douglas DC-10 and Lockheed L-1011

The decline of McDonnell Douglas has been seen by some commentators as the result of unfair competition from Europe. But Tyson paints a different picture: 'Rather, its commercial problems can be traced to more than two decades of undercapitalization and stagnant technology, brought on by its earlier competition with Lockheed', (Tyson, 1992, p. 211). In the US, it was Boeing that won out in the wide-body competition, but even here luck was a key factor, as Boeing's successful move with the jumbo was rather fortuitous. The 747 was not launched as a result of careful market analysis; rather it was a technology-led project, which came about because of Boeing's failure to win the 1960s USAF C-5 competition for a heavy transport aircraft. In 1966, after the competition was lost to Lockheed, Boeing's wide-body design team immediately began work on a commercial version of the planned military transport. Yet the only customer with a clear requirement for this size of aircraft was Pan Am, (Tyson, 1992, p. 186). Ultimately the 747 was very successful, but the decision to launch it was reckless, which, as we argued in Chapter 3, perhaps explains later conservatism at Boeing regarding new product launch.

Conclusion

Airbus's entry into the commercial aircraft market was greeted with great skepticism. With the world economy in the doldrums in the 1970s and the 1973 oil crisis, market conditions could hardly have been more difficult. But through sheer dogged determination Airbus survived the sales desert of the early 1970s and then began to prosper at the expense of its US competitors. The radical concept of the wide-body twin paid dividends as airlines sought to reduce costs.

Not long after the A300 went into service the Airbus management began to see the necessity of the family concept. After the A300 came the A310 and then the A320. With the commercial success of the A320, the technological prowess of the partners had been combined with the political will of the national governments in implementing a game plan that had begun to pay real dividends. In 1986, following on quickly from the A320, Airbus launched the A330/340 program, in order to attack the 747 from below by offering long range aircraft of slightly lower capacity on thinner routes than those where the jumbo was operated.

Figure 4.5   Airbus A330

The A333/340 program finally gave Airbus a family of aircraft to rival Boeing across most of the product range. Also it allowed Airbus to offer its customers significant savings from commonality across the product family, with virtually identical cockpits and similar aircraft handling characteristics. Thus crews could transition from one aircraft type to another after short training courses of just seven or eight days. Maintenance and logistics savings were also achieved because of modular design, allowing rapid installation of interchangeable components. Naturally, none of this was welcomed by Airbus's US competitors, for Airbus was now well positioned to undermine the traditional US dominance. As Figure 4.6 below illustrates Airbus was able to gradually lessen the scale of US dominance.

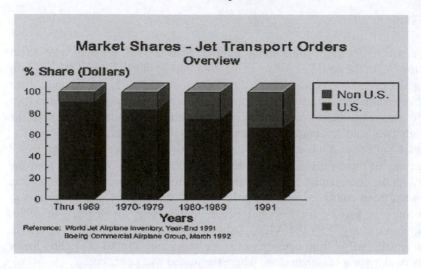

Figure 4.6   The Balance Changes

Chapter 5

Boeing's Response to the A300:
A Tale of Two Models

Introduction

If Boeing Commercial Airplanes (BCA) becomes a case study fixture on the world's MBA courses, then the analysts at top business schools may identify the 1980s as the beginning of Boeing's decline. Yet at the time, the company seemed unassailable. The Boeing 707, 727, 737 and 747 made up the majority of the world's airliner fleet, and McDonnell Douglas (Boeing's closest rival) was in disarray following the DC-10 debacle. Lockheed, the other major US airliner manufacturer, was preparing to exit the civil sector altogether and, while the significance of Europe's Airbus A300 widebody twin had at first been underestimated, Boeing was about to launch two twinjets of its own, the widebody 767 and the narrowbody 757.

In 1980 the 767 had accrued 150 advance orders from the US 'blue chip' carriers, United, American, Delta, and TWA, even though it was not expected to fly until 1982. The 767 looked as though it was another winner and Boeing's main concern was for the 757, its new narrowbody.

Figure 5.1   Boeing 757

The Boeing 757

The 757 was initially conceived as a derivative of the 727 tri-jet, which, after almost 20 years, was the world's most produced airliner. In 1975 an updated and longer-range subtype, the 727-300, had failed to leave the drawing board because of its high unit cost and impending US noise legislation. Boeing refined the design and discarded the 727's rear-engine layout, T-tail, back fuselage, and wing. A new aft-loaded wing carrying two engine pods was the main airframe development. Ultimately, the 757 achieved success with over 1000 sold, but the first ten years of the program were problematic. Moreover, Boeing had expected to sell many more than 1,000 units of an aircraft that had no direct competitor.

The revised configuration promised lower fuel consumption and significantly reduced noise as a result of the high-bypass-ratio engines' lower output velocity and improved nacelle intake and exhaust geometry, technology funded by NASA. However, the Boeing standard-body cabin cross-section of 3.53m (11ft 7in) remained, despite an industry-wide belief that that the days of accommodating 200 passengers in such long and narrow interiors were over. Even before it entered service, the 757 was a curiously anachronistic offering.

FMCS but no Fly-By-Wire

The 757's only real innovation was the Flight Management Computer System (FMCS) it shared with the 767. The decision to incorporate a glass cockpit came at the eleventh hour – the 727's analogue flight deck, cockpit and nose were to have been retained – and meant that the 767's windshield and instrument panel had to be shoehorned into the 757's narrow fuselage. The result was a distinctive but peculiar-looking downward-pointing nose but FMCS enabled a common pilot-type rating, which meant greater flight crew productivity for airlines that operated both models. However, the design disappointed the intended launch customer United, who encouraged McDonnell Douglas to design a competitor (the stillborn DC-X-200). Eventually, the 757 was launched with British Airways and Eastern Airlines.

FMCS was developed in part by Boeing's DoD-funded military divisions, which transferred personnel more used to working on radar and missiles to Seattle's flight deck design team. Dick Taylor, a former BCA vice president, explained 'We needed electronic [sic] people who understood physical databases, and they weren't that prevalent at the time', (Quoted, Becher, 1999, p. 38).

A Small Step Forward

The FMCS system was a significant step forward for Boeing, greatly reducing the pilots' workload as well as flight deck manufacturing time. However, it was not integrated with a fly-by-wire (FBW) control system, which would have greatly increased its capabilities. At the time FBW was revolutionizing fighter aircraft performance and the successful transfer of the technology to the 757 and 767 would have given Boeing a significant direct operating cost advantage over Airbus.

Boeing's failure to seize that opportunity was surprising as it already had a suitable system installed in its YC-14 military transport, the first large aircraft to use a FBW control arrangement. So Boeing was certainly well aware of FBW's possibilities Following the YC-14's cancellation, Boeing had leased the two prototypes from the USAF in order to assess the NASA-developed flight controls. Boeing concluded that FBW would generate many control and inter-relational advantages as well as a 2000 lb reduction in weight, but despite that, the 757 and 767 entered service with conventional hydromechanical systems.

Innate Conservatism

FBW's suitability for large aircraft had been confirmed by the YC-14 but that had not been enough to overcome Boeing's innate conservatism. The company had thrown away its lead in FBW technology, which did not go unnoticed by NASA or the major airlines. Clive Irving, founder of the British *Sunday Times* Insight Team, wrote 'Boeing's inclination, certainly trenchantly expressed by Joe Sutter [the engineer generally credited with the 747], was to leave the pilot with the "feel" of the airplane in his hands', (Irving, 1993, p. 348). Sutter was the executive vice president in charge of Boeing's airliner engineering and development, and had the final say.

After Sutter's retirement in 1986, Boeing began development of a new 'three-lane' FBW system for the 767X project, later to become the 777. By that time Airbus had completed its own electronic flight control system and was in the process of applying it to a whole family of aircraft. The Airbus A320, launched in 1984, is controlled by a FBW system that has since become a landmark in industrial design. Unlike Boeing, Airbus could not ride on the back of a Pentagon program and was obliged to develop its own system architecture. The A320's innovative flight control structure retains a traditional mechanical arrangement for the yaw axis, but uses separate electronic systems to control the pitch and roll axes. Each is able to act as a back-up for the other in the event of a systems failure. Reliability is claimed to be about one failure in ten trillion operations. The lesson was not lost on airlines. Boeing had thrown away its lead in FBW technology not through a failure to realize its significance, but by a simple failure of will.

Mistakes and False Assumptions

The 757 was criticized for its old fashioned structure in which composites were restricted to secondary and non-load bearing parts. Boeing countered that the aircraft's main selling point was fuel efficiency and not profligate new technology. The 757 was designed to have much lower Direct Operating Costs (DOC) than previous generations of jetliners and supposedly could carry 186 passengers on

15% less fuel than a 143-seat 727. However, that calculation did not take into account the fact that approximately half of an airline's DOC stem from an aircraft's purchase price even if fuel prices double, (National Research Council, 1992, pp. 43-44). Suffice to say the 757 was not an inexpensive option, especially given its limited technical capabilities.

Cost of the 757

At its launch in 1982 a 757-200 cost between US$36-42m, whereas a new 727 cost around half as much, (Becher, 1999, p. 46). That price differential meant that the 757-200 was neither faster nor cheaper per seat than the generation of aircraft that came before it. There in a nutshell was the 757's problem: no fiscally responsible airline was going to buy expensive new airliners to replace those it had already had unless they were life-expired. The only other reason why an airline might order new aircraft would be to meet growth, but as a result of the uncertainties created in 1978 by US deregulation, which meant that US domestic airlines were allowed to fly anywhere within the USA and to charge whatever fare they liked, there wasn't any. On top of this the Soviet invasion of Afghanistan in 1979 sparked a huge hike in oil prices. The 757 was off to a bad start.

Design Errors

Boeing's main mistake in the 757's design was conceptual: the assumption that fuel prices could only continue to rise. In 1983 a gallon of fuel cost US$1.20, but by 1986 it costs just 55 cents: the reduction was almost entirely due to Saudi Arabia's increased output of crude oil. The 757-200 was a product of the 1970s and the fuel crisis that followed the Yom Kippur War. The 757 had been designed for fuel efficiency above all else, but by the time it came to market, fuel economy was just one of a number of important purchase criteria. As a result, Boeing's predicted sales of 1400 757-type aircraft by the early 1990s proved wholly inaccurate and just 332 757s were delivered by 1990.

The 757 had other problems. Airlines felt that that it was too big and had unnecessary range. It was a single-aisle aircraft with trans-Atlantic capability. In 1979 USAir publicly complained to Boeing that the 757-200 intended to replace the 727 was now almost as big as its widebody counterpart, the 767-200. Years later, Sutter conceded that a mistake had been made: 'British Airways and Eastern wanted a low-cost airplane and frankly I fought real hard to keep it around 160 seats, but the 757 was pushed closer in capacity to the 767 than we at Boeing wanted', (Quoted, Becher, 1999, p. 30).

Divide and Rule

The fact that Boeing was prepared to compromise the 757 in order to get British Airways onboard the program shows how important Britain was to Boeing's 'divide and rule' strategy for the European aerospace industry. When Eastern Airlines purchased Airbus aircraft in 1978 it brought home to Boeing the potential danger that Airbus represented, even in its home market. Boeing sought to prevent British Aerospace (BAe), the leader in wing design in Europe, from rejoining Airbus and offered to make BAe a risk-sharing subcontractor with responsibility for the 757 wing. Great pressure was put on BAe, both by the carefully timed announcement that British Airways was buying the 757 and the news that the Rolls-Royce RB211 would be the 757 launch engine.

British newspapers, in their typically anti-European manner, hailed the 757 as the chance for a partnership of equals, but it would have been nothing of the sort. BAe, sensing the limitations of the US offer, had no wish to be reduced to a junior partner and opted to join Airbus Industrie instead. In retrospect, British aviation can be seen as the only winner in Boeing's intrigue: British Airways got an aircraft tailored to the particular needs of its intra-European high capacity routes; Rolls-Royce's long-held dream of placing the RB-211 on a Boeing platform was realized; and British Aerospace got a second chance from Airbus just in time for the wing design of the A310. Boeing failed, then, to isolate Britain. But Boeing was to have more success in marginalizing the aerospace industries in Italy and Japan.

The Costs of US Collaboration

Aeritalia (today's Alenia Aerospazio), worked on a number of collaborative ventures with Boeing during the 1970s, none of which came to anything. With precious few aircraft programs of its own, state-owned Aeritalia persuaded the Italian government to invest heavily in new manufacturing plant to make Italy a European centre of excellence for composite structures. Aeritalia became a risk-sharing partner in the 767 in August 1978 and designed and manufactured the aircraft's graphite and Kevlar trailing edge components, as well as the nose radome. By 1982 the Italian government had invested US$94m in the program and the new composites plant was capable of producing 12 767 part sets per month. Aeritalia expected to break even after shipping 500 sets but with less than 300 767s sold by the end of 1989, the program was unsuccessful and much of its expensive plant lay idle, (Birtles, 1999, pp. 19-20).

The Japanese Gambit

Boeing's relationship with Japan was of particular importance to the company and is still in place today. As we saw in Chapter 3, in the dark days of 1971, Boeing even considered selling the whole 737 operation to Japan. Japan is one of Boeing's biggest markets and has been since the days when airlines were encouraged by the government to buy Boeing in order to reduce Japan's embarrassing trade surplus with the United States. However, Japan has airliner design and manufacturing ambitions of its own and, during the 1960s and 1970s, built two indigenous transport aircraft, the NAMC YS-11 turboprop airliner and the Kawasaki C1 twin-jet military airlifter. Neither had much impact outside Japan and so the Civil Transport Development Corporation (CTDC) was formed to become risk-sharing sub-contractors on the 767.

A key Japanese objective was to gain tacit knowledge and technology transfer but Boeing kept the more challenging manufacturing procedures to itself and left CTDC with the fuselage barrel, the wing-to-fuselage fairings and the main landing gear doors. Boeing offered a collaborative venture, the 7J7 propfan, as compensation but it did not leave the drawing board; as with the Sonic Cruiser many years later, it is still unclear whether it was ever intended to.

Today CTDC is known as Commercial Airplane Company, or CAC, and comprises Japan's leading aerospace companies Fuji, Kawasaki, and Mitsubishi. CAC manufactures most of the 767 fuselage barrel, its wing-to-fuselage fairings and the main landing gear doors. Its share of the 767 program amounts to 15%, but Japanese companies have also gained much of the non-American equipment contracts. Thus, despite the lack of technology transfer, the Japanese seem to feel that the 767 provides an effective showcase for their work and have since been involved in a number of other Boeing programs, notably the 777 and the 787.

Boeing 767: 2-4-2 or 2-3-2?

The fuselage cross-section of a large commercial aircraft is arguably the most important aspect of its design. A wing or engine may be replaced if necessary but a cross-section once in production is very difficult to change. The 757's designers at Renton were not required to give much thought to its cross-section; they were obliged to use the standard body ellipse established by the 707. The Everett design team did not have it so easy; the cross-section of the existing Boeing widebody, the 747, was far too large to be used by the 767 and a completely new cabin had to be developed.

Figure 5.2   Boeing 767

Everett examined the cross-section of the Airbus A300B, then the only widebody twin in service. After much deliberation, Airbus had arrived at a width of 18ft 6in (5.67m), as it allowed eight abreast seating (2-4-2) plus underfloor storage for two LD3s, the industry standard cargo container in use with the L-1011 and DC-10. (The larger Boeing 747 could accommodate LD3s or LD1s.) In 1976 Boeing praised the Airbus cross-section during discussions about a possible collaborative aircraft venture, so there was much surprise when it announced that the 767 would have a 16ft 6in (5.03m) cross-section and seven abreast seating (2-3-2).

Some 40 airlines were consulted before the 767 design was finalized and most expressed a clear preference for eight-abreast seating, yet Boeing had selected a cabin body 2ft (0.61m) narrower than that of Airbus. Boeing argued that seven abreast seating would mean that no passenger was more than one seat away from an aisle, but as the A300 or A310's cabins could be configured for 2-3-2, no one took that explanation seriously. Bill Gunston claims that a member of the Everett team later admitted, 'We couldn't select the same figure as Airbus and decided on less rather than more', (Gunston, 1998, p. 135).

The choice of such a narrow cross-section caused immense damage to the 767 and hindered its acceptance in the market. Allegedly, the aircraft had to be heavily discounted to overcome its negative reputation. One crucial factor was that the hold was unable to accommodate LD3 containers side by side, an essential capability for airlines requiring direct cargo transfer capability with other widebody types. Boeing concentrated on optimizing the 767's suitability for US trunk routes where cargo was not a major consideration, but it was of great importance to many overseas airlines, especially in the so-called Tiger Economies, and during the 1980s many Boeing customers in the Pacific Rim opted for the Airbus A310 and A300 over the 767.

Questions were also raised about the 767's oversize wing, which United, the launch customer, demanded to get in and out of the high-altitude airports in its network. The wing's weight badly compromised the first 767-200 variant, which consequently did not have a long production life. However, it was to prove ideal for the heavier extended-range 767s that were later introduced.

767 ETOPS

Although the 767-200 was sized to suit the home market, in 1982 US orders collapsed before the aircraft had even entered service. The continuing economic recession and the air traffic control chaos caused by President Reagan's dismissal of air traffic controllers were contributory factors, but the aircraft's lack of range was also significant.

The 767 program was salvaged in the late 1980s by the Extended-range Twin Engine Operations (ETOPS) revolution, for which Boeing is usually credited. Today it is largely forgotten that in 1982 the company was reluctant to produce a long-range 767, fearing it would cannibalize sales of the highly profitable 747. It was only when the 767's sales died that Boeing decided to go ahead with the 767ER (Extended Range) which was launched in January 1983, quickly followed by the 767-300 in September that year.

The 767-300 had intercontinental range and a fuselage stretch of 21 ft (6.4m) , which meant up to 40 more passengers. Those improvements were enough to make the -300 the most popular 767 subtype; its first customer was JAL, clearly under pressure from the Japanese government and CTDC. As ETOPS was extended, by 1988 the 767 sales picture began to improve. Joe Sutter believes that:

> The idea of using twins over water came from the Boeing gang. It was a carefully thought-out process. Selling it first to the certifying authorities and then to the public was ... a tough job. At the time, everyone liked to look and see four engines out there. We determined that twins over water were a natural ... We were looking at what the plane [767] could do, at least to make it a good North Atlantic airplane, (Quoted, Becher, p. 28).

The ETOPS Myth

The Boeing version of ETOPS history quoted above is widely accepted even though Eastern Airlines used Airbus A300s for flights over the Caribbean in the 1970s. Back then it was also not uncommon for European cargo operators, such as Hapag Lloyd, to fly A300s across the Atlantic. It was these flights that proved the technical feasibility of operating twins over water. Boeing's achievement was to persuade the US Federal Aviation Administration (FAA) to extend its archaic FAR Part 121.161, which required that any US twin flying across water had to be within 60 minutes of a diversionary airfield. Boeing and TWA conducted a number of proving flights until the FAA accepted that modern engines were sufficiently reliable for twins to be 90 minutes away from a diversionary airfield. Subsequently, as a result of Boeing pressure on the FAA, the ETOPS limits have been pushed up to, first 180 minutes and ultimately 207 minutes, to facilitate the 777's Asia Pacific operations.

The FAA was well aware that Boeing's sales would benefit from the ETOPS extensions as its large wing gave the 767 a considerable range advantage over the A300-600R and the A310. Nevertheless, Airbus supported Boeing's efforts to extend ETOPS diversionary times as the performance envelopes of Airbus's twinjets were also extended. However, it is interesting to note that when Airbus began to design the A340 ultra long-range aircraft, it specified four engines rather than two; Boeing decided that less was more and the 777, once announced as a tri-jet, became a twin.

The End of the 757 and 767?

More than two decades later the exact cost of the 757 and 767 programs is still unclear. In 1998 the aviation economist R.E.G. Davies suggested that the aircraft cost US$3 billion each to develop and in the absence of official figures this seems a reasonable estimate, (Davies, 1998. p. 49). Boeing is said to have spent US$2.5 billion on expanding the Renton and Everett manufacturing and assembly sites, including US$500m on Computer Numerical Control (CNC)[1] plant: that expenditure may be included in Davies's calculations, (Becher, p. 41). No details of the Japanese government's financial contribution to the 767 appear to have been made generally available.

The final 757 was delivered in April 2005 reflecting the 'market reality for the 757', which could no longer compete with the much younger Airbus A321, (Boeing, October 2003). A total of 1,050 were made, making the 757 the sixth biggest selling jetliner in history, an impressive achievement given its poor sales performance during the 1980s. (Its sales boom came late in life as US airlines replaced their time-expired 727s.) A breakdown of these figures reveals that more than 700 of these orders were from US operators. This reflects a trend seen in most of Boeing's current family of aircraft: they sell better in America and Japan than the rest of the world.

Since 2000 it has become clear that the 767 is also approaching the end of its production life, though no official announcement has yet been made. In the 1990s, Airbus's A300-600 and A310 were reinforced by the A330-200, which is a fierce and successful competitor to both the 767 and the 777. Despite this, it was hoped to keep the 767 production line going with the projected KC-767 tanker deal with the USAF, worth US$23.5 billion. However, following procurement irregularities involving Boeing personnel, the US Congress killed off the lease deal.

---

[1] Numerical Control factories were another benefit provided to American industry by the US Air Force, (Noble, 1987, p. 340).

Nevertheless, Boeing still hope to sell KC-767s to the USAF so the 767 may yet pass the magic 1000 units sales figure and help keep BCA in business until the 787 arrives.

Conclusion

The 757 and 767 were a response to Airbus's A300 and A310. After difficult starts, both went on to achieve good sales figures. However, they were not successful enough to prevent many airlines, particularly those outside the USA, from switching from Boeing aircraft to Airbus products, despite the product support and training complications such a move entailed.

As the newcomer Airbus found it difficult, but not impossible, to challenge Boeing's market position. The widebody twin concept was copied by Boeing on the 767, but not with sufficient effect to kill off the A300, which has now reached nearly 600 units sold, more than both the DC-10 and the L-1011, (*Flight International*, 26 October, 2004, p. 51). So, in other words, Airbus's first product was good enough to beat the offerings of the number two and three players in the US and also eat into the market share of the number one, Boeing.

So what went wrong for BCA? How did Airbus successfully challenge the incumbent? The truth is Boeing got some of the technical decisions wrong. The aviation axiom that if you get the cross-section of an airliner wrong, it doesn't matter what else you get right, was borne out by the 757 and 767. There seems little doubt that if the 767 had had a wider cross-section it would have been a significantly more difficult aircraft for Airbus Industrie to counter, given its greater 'stretch' and longer range. (The 767's replacement, the 787, will have a significantly wider cabin.)

Boeing's sales figures show that the 767 outsold the A310 by a ratio of three-to-one. However, that is a deliberate distortion of the data as the 767-300 is nearer in size to the A300B/A300-600R. Once the sales for these two Airbus subtypes are factored in we can see that the sales war was very close indeed.

Table 5.1 A300/A310 and 767 Sales

Type	A300	767-300	A310	767-200
Sales	589	618	260	248
Total	Airbus		Boeing	
	849		866	

Source: *Flight International,* 26 October 2004.

Epilogue

As we saw in Chapter 3, in 1985 BCA launched the 747-400, a heavily revised version of its monopoly product, which took three years to bring to market. At the end of the 1980s it was the major contributor to record BCA revenues of US$8 billion, which generated an operating profit of US$317m or just 4.7%. The return on Boeing's defense sales, such as the AGM-86B cruise missile, was nearly twice as much.

With sales of the new 757 and 767 aircraft below expectations, Boeing concluded its capital could be more profitably employed developing new non-airliner products and, like MDC before it, decided to concentrate on derivatives of its existing family of airliners. It is arguable that that decision, more than any of the shortcomings of the 757 and 767 outlined here, was ultimately the most damaging to BCA's long-term prospects. It was certainly the beginning of the end for Boeing as the market leader in large commercial aircraft.

Chapter 6

Boeing: The Flight from Innovation

Reprise: Boeing's Dominance and the Airbus Challenge

Through a combination of good management, good fortune and government support, Boeing, with its 707 series jets, secured a pivotal position during the early years of commercial jet aviation. This provided the launch pad for Boeing's 35 years of market domination in the commercial jet aircraft sector. The 707 was followed-up aggressively in the 1960s with the successful 727, 737 and 747 series aircraft, these types capturing 'pole positions' respectively, in the short range and long-haul markets throughout the world. Year on year, Boeing achieved growth in market share at the expense of other US manufacturers and of the nationally-based European aerospace firms as they each declined to the point of extinction in the civil aircraft marketplace. By the 1970s Boeing was not only the biggest global player in commercial aviation; it had also virtually become the monopoly supplier in large passenger jets – long haul in particular. But as we saw in Chapter 5, Boeing's response to the A300, in the shape of the 757/767 was not entirely convincing and left some airlines disappointed. Although the 757 eventually sold well, it faced no direct competitor until the arrival of the A321 and therefore its real quality is difficult to gauge. In the 737/A320 battle the picture is clearer. Airbus's single aisle A320 family took the market by storm and in 2003 became the most common aircraft type in the world fleet, (*Flight International,* 1 September, 2003). As of October 2004 the A320 series had sold 3,256 units, (*Flight International,* 26 October, 2004).

Since the 757/767 era, Boeing has become highly conservative, clearly not wanting to repeat the risky experience of the 747. As we show in the argument developed below, this is the key reason for Boeing's relative decline in the market place and its loss of the number one position to Airbus. It has failed to launch new products, apart from the 777 and, more recently, the 787. But even the prelude to the 777 saw Boeing trying to offer its customers yet another derivative of the 767. Between 1986 and 1988 Boeing executives flew around the world trying to sell the world's airlines a new variant 767. As Karl Sabbagh illustrates the Boeing team, led by John Roundhill, eventually got the message: 'For two years, in a constant shuttle between Boeing and its customers, men with briefcases spread out the latest variant of the 767 in front of the airline executives, and went away, tail between their legs, armed with reasons why this model solved one problem, but introduced another', (Sabbagh, 1996, p. 21).

Boeing's Complacency

By the late 1960s the civil aerospace sector in Europe had been battered yet it did not surrender to the US manufacturers. As we saw in Chapter 4, after the learning experience of Concorde, and despite its commercial failure, Airbus was born. From the late 1960s, Boeing observed the nascent Airbus and its precursor European companies with a detached and rather complacent air, as they embarked first on the A300 and then the development of a new range of civil aircraft under the Airbus Industrie name. From the US companies perspective there was seemingly nothing to be concerned about in the early part of this period. After a shaky start the Boeing 747 had built up a virtual monopoly position in the long haul, wide-body market and every reputable intercontinental carrier in the free world would eventually take delivery of the ubiquitous 'Jumbo'. In the meantime the Boeing 737 had become the staple airliner for the short sector 120-seat plus market, operating inter-national, inter-city and island hopping routes across every continent in the world outside the Iron Curtain.

Boeing, comfortable in its top position, clearly did not read the signs in the market place correctly. If Boeing executives had looked more carefully then they would have seen that there were warning signs about Airbus's potential as early as 1979, when Airbus sold more wide-bodies than the American company, (Heppenheimer, 1995, p. 298). In reality it should have come as no surprise that a European challenge would be serious. After all, almost all the key innovations in aeronautics had come from Europe and in 1939 Germany led the world. But the threat was underestimated and subsequently, an undue emphasis on the subsidy issue has led to a failure to focus on what is arguably the key issue: it is through investment in new product, and building aircraft that customers want, that Airbus has prevailed. The critical failure at Boeing has been the failure to invest in genuinely new programs, plus major exogenous managerial failures, such as the manufacturing crisis of 1998 and the political imbroglio of 2003.

From Oligopoly to Duopoly

After the disastrous experience of the L-1011, Lockheed dropped out of the civil market in 1981, only ten years after being rescued by a Federal loan guarantee of US$250m, (Mowery, 1987, p. 39). By the early 1990s McDonnell-Douglas (MDC) was also in trouble. On the one hand MDC was being squeezed on the commercial front by Airbus and Boeing, on the other hand the end of the Cold War meant drastic cuts in its defense business. Orders for the KC-10 tanker in the 1980s and the C-17 transporter in the 1990s helped MDC survive, but in the commercial market everything depended on the MD-11; a stretch of the DC-10 with new avionics and systems technology. But sadly for the Long Beach-based company the MD-11 also flopped. Performance deficiencies, particularly in the promised range, with shortfalls of up to 600 nautical miles, plagued the aircraft and irritated the main launch customer, American Airlines, (Norris & Wagner, 1999, p. 66). Yet again engineering had not delivered on the commitments made by marketing. Although the MD-11 eventually made good as a freighter, the commercial failure of the aircraft was another 'nail in the coffin' for MDC.

Lockheed survived by refocusing its aircraft capabilities almost entirely on the defense business sector with military airlifters and fighters. McDonnell Douglas 'soldiered on' with a relatively restricted range of MD-series commercial aircraft supported by a strong defense business. However, having been eliminated from the crucial Joint Strike Fighter program in late 1996, MDC could no longer survive as an independent manufacturer in commercial or defense aerospace. In 1997 it merged with – or rather was swallowed by – Boeing in a controversial US$13.9 billion takeover. With the demise of the famous name of Douglas as a force in commercial aviation, the last remaining products in the MD line were re-designated as Boeing aircraft. From then on the world's large commercial aircraft industry was a duopoly.

Airbus's Rise

Airbus first broke into the US domestic market with sales of the A300 aircraft to Eastern Airlines. Through the late 1970s market success was slow in coming, but in the 1980s events changed dramatically. By 1985 the A300/A310 was taking 44.5% of the widebody market, with McDonnell Douglas at just 2.5%, (Lynn, 1997, p. 168). Such success was followed with sales of single-aisle A320s to Pan Am and Northwest in the late 1980s. These sales were critical, as the large US market was hostile to non-American manufactured aircraft. In the 1980s the balance was clearly changing, with Airbus moving to a 30% market share by the early 1990s and the number two spot in world sales rankings.

A Relentless Challenge

It was seemingly not until the 1990s that the real seriousness of the challenge from Airbus became evident to Boeing. Public statements by Boeing executives revealed a profound sense of shock when numerous US carriers, such as US Airways, began placing large orders for Airbus aircraft, rather than supporting their traditional Seattle-based supplier. In terms of orders, by the turn of the century, the market had been transformed from a Boeing-dominated oligopoly to a roughly equal duopoly, with Airbus fractionally in the lead.

Table 6.1   Airbus/Boeing Deliveries and Backlog

	Boeing			Airbus		
Aircraft Deliveries	Single Aisle	Large Intermediate Aircraft	Total	Single Aisle	Large Intermediate Aircraft	Total
2000	358	131	489	236	75	311
2001	393	134	527	255	70	325
2002	272	109	234	234	69	303
2003	199	82	233	233	72	305
2004	214	71	233	233	87	320
Backlog	1097			1500		

Aircraft Deliveries for 2000-2003 and Order Backlog at 31 December, 2003, (http://www.speednews.com).

In 2000 Airbus shared the market with Boeing on equal terms, but has since edged ahead. The battle was won first in orders for new aircraft. In 2002 Airbus secured 375 sales, compared to Boeing's 329, but gradually Airbus has also moved to parity in deliveries. In 2003, for the first time, Airbus delivered more aircraft than Boeing. The Airbus backlog is now also significantly larger than that of the U.S. company. Recent aircraft deliveries and sales backlog figures set out in the table above show clearly how the virtual monopoly position enjoyed by Boeing 25 years ago has been turned round. Even more worrying for both Boeing and its customers is the fact that in 2004 backlog orders for four of the company's products were dangerously low. As of 30 September 2004 the total backlog for 747-400, 757, 767 and 717 was just 95 units (www.speednews.com). The 757 line closed in October 2004 and the 717 will end production during 2006 leaving question marks over the future of both the 747-400 and 767. It is a stark fact that, for the present, the survival of Boeing Commercial Airplanes largely depends on just two products, the 777 and the 737 Next Generation, with the 787 some years away.

Airbus Growth, the US Aerospace Industry and Boeing's Response

With the emergence and steady growth of Airbus from 1970 onwards, US commercial aeronautics was faced with a slow but steady decline in its share of the world commercial aircraft market. In the early 1990s the US aerospace industry was also hit by drastic reductions in defense procurement. It responded, in the main, with a program of rationalization, mergers, joint ventures and various types of international subcontracting arrangements. The rationalizations and mergers, in some cases orchestrated by the US Department of Defense, gathered pace with inevitable consequences, with Boeing ending up in the dominant position, as table 6.2 below clearly reveals. Eventually, the other remaining player on the civil side, McDonnell-Douglas (MDC) lost critical mass in market share taking just 5% in 1996, (Lynn, 1997, p. 226). As a result it could no longer afford to develop or improve its product ranges. In consequence it was absorbed by Boeing in 1997. In the immediate post merger situation Boeing described itself as follows:

> The Boeing Company, based in Seattle, Washington, is the largest aerospace company in the world, as measured by total sales, and the nation's leading exporter. Boeing is the world's largest manufacturer of commercial jetliners and military aircraft, and the nation's largest NASA contractor. The company's capabilities in aerospace also include helicopters, electronic and defense systems, missiles, rocket engines, launch vehicles, and advanced information and communication systems. The company has an extensive global reach with customers in 145 countries and operations in 27 US states. At year-end 1998, Boeing and its subsidiaries employed approximately 231,000 people, (Boeing Annual Report, 1998).

Despite the creation of the new Boeing and the rationalization of the American defense/aerospace industrial base, the decline in civil sales continued and the US share of world commercial jet sales fell below 50% in both 1999 and 2001. The trend has also continued in the recent past. In 2003 Airbus won 53.19% of orders placed, but more significantly had a much larger share of orders by value, (*The Economist,* 29 November, 2003, p. 85).

Table 6.2   The 1999 Post-Mergers Aerospace Ranking by Sales (US$bn)

Rank	Country	Company	US$bn
1	USA	Boeing/McDonnell Douglas	55.4
2	USA	Lockheed Martin	26
3	EU	EADS (Includes CASA)	21.8
4	UK	BAE Systems	20.5
5	USA	Raytheon	17.5
6	USA	United Technologies	12
7	USA	General Electric	10.3
8	USA	Honeywell	9.8
9	USA	Northrop Grumman	9.1
10	USA	TRW	5.9

Source: *Flight International,* 8-14 September 1999 and 20-26 October 1999.

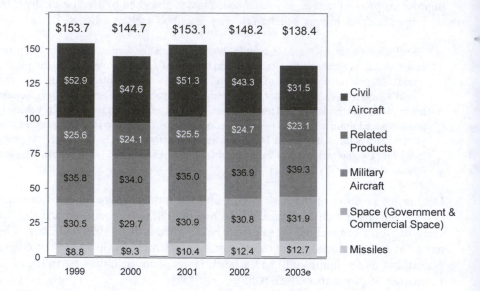

Figure 6.1   The Decline in US Commercial Aircraft Sales (US$bn)
Credit: US AIA.

But even this does not represent anything like the full story. In order even to sustain this declining share, Boeing had increasingly turned to 'offset' or international outsourcing arrangements where a segment of the manufacturing work is transferred to the buyer nation, both as a marketing incentive and a method of driving down production costs through transferring sub-assembly work to emerging low labour-cost countries. While Boeing is not alone in offering international manufacturing offsets to buyer countries, the extent to which it has turned to this type of arrangement is considerably greater than that of Airbus. Moreover, Boeing has been prepared increasingly to countenance this type of arrangement on its newer products. For example, in the 1970s the Boeing 727 had some 2% foreign content in its manufacture, whereas in the 1990s there was almost 30% foreign manufacturing content in the Boeing 777, (Pritchard, 2002, p. 3). As we illustrate below this trend has gone even further on the new 787.

Boeing's Business Strategy and Product Development

Having attained its near monopoly position in the 1970s and 80s and despite its public relations slogan – *forever new frontiers* – Boeing has been inclined to rely on a strategy of cost competitiveness, derivatives development and product evolution, rather than technological advancement, as its favoured way of consolidating market share. Moreover, having flirted with a supersonic transport but having also witnessed the economic failure of the Anglo-French Concorde, perhaps there seemed little incentive, in Boeing's opinion, to push for advanced technologies. In the Boeing view, the airframe and systems technologies available in the 1970s were adequate, with modest evolutionary development added to serve the established subsonic but growing, high-volume market. To meet the demands of the time, chiefly for cheaper international travel, while showing concern for the environment, Boeing was able to rely on the fierce competition underway between the big jet engine manufacturers, engaged in developing more fuel-efficient, reliable and quieter engines. Incorporating these engines into its derivative jets enabled Boeing to sell improved operational economics without excessive technical and cost risk to itself. Moreover, with the emergence of very reliable engines and the growth of Extended-range Twin-engine Operations (ETOPS), Boeing was able to retain and grow market share simply by improving production methods and generally optimising its product range through derivative developments, to meet the demands of the market.

Destroying Value: the Derivative Years

From a business point of view the timing of the introduction of the twinjet families, 757, 767 and later the 777 was impeccable, even if the 757 and 767 had significant design shortcomings. Each was introduced as the ETOPS concept developed and expanded so that Boeing was able to offer aircraft ideally suited to the developing market. Moreover, and to the delight of its shareholders, it was able to do so without accommodating significant technical risk. However, those good years are now in the past. Boeing is now exposed in the marketplace with an ageing and relatively low technology model range (with the exception of the 777) and, in recent years, has shown little appetite for the major investment needed to recover from that situation.

Controversially, the 787 is going ahead with more than US$5.5bn of subsidy from the States of Washington and Kansas and the governments of Japan and Italy. And yet ironically it is Boeing who prompted the US government to bring a World Trade Organization (WTO) subsidies case against Airbus in September 2004. Regarding the funding of a new product range, BAE Systems outgoing chairman, Sir Richard Evans, suggested in 2004 that Boeing would need to spend between US$40-US$50 billion over the next 10 to 15 years if it wants to match Airbus's product range, (*The Financial Times*, 27 February 2004).

The four generic aircraft types in the current Boeing product range have all been highly successful in economic and airline business terms. They have served both Boeing and its shareholders well. But of these four generic types, the 737 and 747 were designed in the 1960s and the 767 is a 1970s design. Of the present Boeing product range, only the 777 (with development support worth US$942m from the Japanese) and the latest 'next-generation' derivatives of the 737, could be considered marketable, state-of-the-art commercial jets that fully meet today's market requirements. To underscore the point, since 1980 Boeing has launched 20 derivatives or variants within the Boeing family, but of these 13 have been derivatives of 1960s designed jets. This short-term approach served Boeing well financially during the last 25 years of the 20th century, but has left the company poorly placed for the demands of the 21st century.

Destroying Strategic Value

To return to the main theme of this study Boeing has neglected the issue of *strategic value*. Short-term commitment to good financial returns is not the same as securing long term strategic viability. In the 1990s Boeing's annual reports mention 'value', almost as a mantra. But the concept of value is clearly a narrow cash-based one related to stock price. It is not the concept of strategic value proposed in the argument of this book. In an extraordinary move in 1999-2001 Boeing spent US$8 billion to buy back its own shares. CEO Phil Condit proclaimed in a news release that, 'Our solid performance, strong backlog, and robust cash flow' were the reasons for the share buyback. In fact 2000 was a record year for the company with billions in cash flow. But investing in stock, when new product is required, privileges shareholders at the cost of employees and customers.

The 1998 Annual Report proclaims: 'Value - providing the most gain for the least cost - has become the big driver in everything we do. Anywhere and everywhere, the challenge is: *'How can we provide better value?'* In the same report can be found, 'Shareholder value is the single most important measure of our long-term success. To create superior returns to shareholders, *we are now looking at every single program with an eye towards maximising value*. Nothing will escape scrutiny, and we are focused on fixing or eliminating those programs which destroy value', (Boeing Annual Report 1998). But these statements are oriented to stock value. Looked at from a different perspective the money used in the share buy-back could have financed a new product. But the stock buyback has not finished. In October 2004 CEO Harry Stonecipher explained that increased earnings in 2004 would also be used in 2005 to buy back more Boeing stock, (www.smartmoney.com, 27 October 2004).

Boeing appears to have taken to relatively short-term thinking, and developed a real aversion to funding the launch of new products. This is in spite of the competition from Airbus, which now has a complete homogeneous family of modern airplanes. By concentrating on derivatives Boeing has squandered billions of dollars on their development, which has done nothing for the company's long-term future and also provided no catalyst to advance the technological competence of the supplier industry. Looking at the matter from the perspective of the US national interest, one could argue that the failure to invest in new technology and new programs has degraded Boeing's strategic value to the country. Seen in that light its failure to win the Joint Strike Fighter (JSF) contest against Lockheed Martin in 2001 seems hardly surprising. Perhaps more significantly, the failure to invest in new product is reducing the attraction of the sector to graduate engineers and undermining the skill base of the aerospace industry in the USA. According to

MacPherson and Pritchard, 450,000 science and engineering jobs were lost in the US aerospace industry between 1970 and 2000, (MacPherson and Pritchard, 2004, p. 6). John Douglas, president of the American Aerospace Industries Association (AIA), has testified to the US Congress that the average age of a US aerospace engineer is now 54 and also explained that only 2% of engineering graduates now enter the aerospace sector in the US, (MacPherson and Pritchard, 2004, p. 6). Failure to invest in new product easily translates into a perceived lack of belief in the future of the industry and seemingly this is the message being transmitted to America's aerospace workforce.

Federal Support

The failure at Boeing to invest in new products is certainly not because of a lack of financial support from Federal agencies. In the 1990s, NASA ran two huge Research and Technology (R&T) Programs to help Boeing find and develop a new aircraft concept. The High Speed Research (HSR) program was designed to launch a new US supersonic vehicle, while the Advanced Subsonic Technology (AST) program was oriented towards the conventional civil jetliner. Having played a key role in the development of the 777, NASA wanted to promote a new air vehicle for the 21st century and help the US recapture the initiative. As Wesley Harris, NASA's Associate Administrator, explained to the House of Representatives:

> NASA's objective in the Advanced Subsonic Technology program is to provide US industry with a competitive edge to recapture market share, maintain a strongly positive balance of trade, and increase US jobs', (Testimony to the House of Representative, 10 February 1994).

Table 6.3   NASA Aeronautical Research and Technology Program Budget (US$m)

	FY93	FY94	FY95	FY96	FY97	FY98	FY93 - 98
R&T Base	436.5	448.3	366.3	354.7	404.2	418.3	2428.3
AST	12.4	101.3	150.1	169.8	173.6	211.1	818.3
HSR	117.0	187.2	221.3	233.3	243.1	245.0	1246.9
Other	299.7	83.9	144.3	159.5	23.3	45.7	756.4
TOTAL	865.6	820.7	882.0	917.3	844.2	920.1	5249.9

Source: NASA Budget 1999.

Table 6.3 above shows the public funding for potential new programs. The aim is clear: 'The National Aeronautics and Space Administration (NASA) funds the development of technology and systems intended for use in commercial airliners –

both subsonic and supersonic – with the explicit objective of preserving the US share of the current and future world airliner market', (Congress of United States Budget Office, Reducing the Deficit: Spending and Revenue Options, A Report to the Senate and House Committees on the Budget, 152, February 1995). But as well as the vehicle related projects vast sums were spent on the R&T Base program, which in the past has provided the following technologies for US aircraft:

> Supercritical Wing for the 757 and 767;
> Winglets for the MD-11 and 747-400;
> Acoustic nacelles for the MD-11, 757, 767, and 747;
> Active turbine cooling for the JT9D engine and the 747;
> Composite structures and aluminium alloys for the 757, 767, 747 and the MD-11;
> Advanced flight decks for the 757, 767, 747 & 777.

(NASA Office of Aeronautics, FY 1996 Budget Report)

Despite this support Boeing did not launch a new program. Even for some commentators in the US this was unpalatable. The *New York Times* noted, 'After NASA poured US$1.6 billion into a risky effort to help Boeing Co develop a revolutionary supersonic jetliner, the Seattle based aerospace giant has decided not to build it', (*New York Times*, 6 February 1999).

Technological Conservatism

While Airbus was staking its future on advanced technologies to develop a position in the future commercial aircraft markets there were no significant leaps forward in Boeing's airframe technologies. That is not to suggest that design improvements were not on the agenda at all at Boeing. Boeing took advantage of improvements in materials technologies and developed its flight sciences capabilities to provide sound improvements in flight performance. However, the bold step taken by Airbus in the 1980s into 'fly-by-wire' control technologies was not adopted by Boeing at that time. Indeed, the company showed considerable reticence before investing in 'fly-by-wire' and digital control technologies for civil aircraft. It was more than ten years behind Airbus in this technological 'leap of faith'. In Boeing's view, the benefits did not justify the technical and cost risks at the time of Airbus's first venture into such technologies.

It was not until development of the 777 that Boeing embarked on its first steps into commercial aircraft fly-by-wire (Sabbagh, 1995). The 777 is the newest commercial aircraft program on Boeing's books and remains its only commercial product employing FBW technology. The story on the use of composite materials for the airframe is similar. The 777 represented the first significant use of composites in a Boeing commercial design with around 12% of the airframe comprising composites.

Having taken these first tentative steps with the 777, Boeing is now proposing 50% composite materials content in the 787 program (*Flight International*, 7-13 January 2003). It is also adopting a more electric aircraft approach to systems design and a significant reduction in hydraulics and pneumatics in future products, as a step towards lower operating and maintenance costs. In short, although it is now beginning to embrace new technologies, its developments over the last 25 years have been characterized by an evolution of existing technology and cost-focussed product optimization.

Market Outlook and Forecasting

Over the last 10 to 12 years, with Airbus challenging it in every market, and beating it in many, Boeing has been forced to take a hard look at its products, the technologies they offer and the demands of the market. There are some indications that Boeing now recognizes the need to take a much bolder line in adopting new technologies, to enable it to offer reduced airplane direct operating costs and to win back customers. The 777 went only part of the way to redressing the technology deficit it has against comparable Airbus products. Having claimed a large degree of success with the 777, Boeing now claims to be ready to take bolder steps forward in technology on its next product. However, its business strategy depends to just as great an extent on its forecasts for future aircraft sales, as it does on new technologies. In particular, much rests on the accuracy of its forecasts for the relative numbers of large, intermediate sized and regional jets to be purchased by the airlines over the next 20 years.

Boeing's forecasts over the last ten years for the future of commercial aviation have been characterized by two quite specific concepts, (Boeing, *Current Market Outlook,* 2001, 2002, 2003, http://www.boeing.com/commercial).

These can be summarized as follows:

> ➢ Passengers in the future will prefer the convenience and speed of travel offered by more frequent and direct services (even over long ranges) in preference to the 'hub and spoke' mode, which has characterized the last 40 years of commercial air travel development.

> ➢ Competition across carriers would demand ever-lower direct operating costs, higher revenues per passenger mile, while aircraft would have to become more environmentally friendly.

Constraints on the Boeing Philosophy

The problem with the first view expressed above is that 80% of passengers travel in economy and are clearly not willing to pay a premium for speed. Moreover, overall journey time is often more a function of the travel and logistics either end of the actual flight. Since 9/11 this has become even more the case as laborious but necessary security processes are now required.

While few would argue with the second of these asserted philosophies, the first is, arguably, also not supported by any significant trend or change in the pattern of passenger traffic growth. Moreover, the idea of more frequent 'city-pairs' services is, to some degree, in conflict with the economic and environmental objectives recognized in the second conceptual market driver. Proposals for new airport developments and more frequent take-offs and landings raise ever-more intense environmental objections everywhere they are tabled throughout the world. Cramming more aircraft and flights into existing facilities, lengthening the flight operations day, building new runways and all of the necessary support infrastructure has become a planning nightmare. One solution to this is the use of less frequent flights between the big hubs and spoke-to-hub, using bigger and more environmentally friendly aircraft, such as Airbus's A380. To take just one example, three A380 aircraft can carry more passengers than four Boeing 747-400s, thus freeing up airport slots.

Nevertheless, and despite any contrary evidence, over the last five years, Boeing's belief in the mid-size twin-aisle aircraft market has intensified, as has its assertion that the market demand for very large aeroplanes (747/A380) will gradually decline. Boeing believes that intermediate sized aircraft are inherently more flexible and with new technologies would be capable of serving long-range intercontinental markets, as well as high-density intermediate-range markets with lower operating economics. Boeing also contends that the demand will grow for more frequent direct point-to-point services, bypassing the big capital city hubs characterizing today's airline routes. This concept has formed a common thread through Boeing's market outlook over a number of years now, particularly since completion of development and introduction into service of the 777. But it should be born in mind that the world's largest airlines have invested huge amounts of money in their hub operations, where their maintenance and other logistics are most cost-effectively carried out. Thus the aircraft manufacturer's major customers have their own reasons not to want the aviation system to become too fragmented.

Mixed Messages

Despite the point-to-point concept there have been confusing and mixed messages from Boeing, in terms of its new product proposals. Although seemingly focused on developing an aircraft concept of suitable size and range to replace the ageing 767, to provide the point-to-point service it believes will appeal to the future passenger market, Boeing also at one stage proposed growth versions of the 747-

400, the 747X and 747X-Stretch. These proposals were probably designed, as much as anything else, in an attempt to damage the prospects for the proposed Airbus A3XX (now the A380) by trying to lure 747-400 operators away from the proposed A380. Some in Boeing's management believed that they could, if nothing else, de-stabilize the A380 program while retaining what was left, in their view, of a diminishing market for outsize commercial passenger transport aircraft.

The real problem for Boeing was that A380 showed significant performance improvements over the 747 that have been brought about by the embodiment of advanced airframe build techniques and materials, aircraft systems and propulsion technologies. These advances, which include more use of lighter composite materials and advanced alloys, will enable the A380 to break even with a load factor of less than 59% compared with 70% on the 747-400. Thus, although Boeing was not convinced of the market and was therefore never enthusiastic about the outlay of the relatively modest funds (compared with Airbus's A380 investment), in the final analysis it was offering an inferior product. The 747X was therefore eventually abandoned. Even Boeing's close Japanese strategic partners did not like the 747X concept and the proposed Japanese partners refused to commit funds to the new project, arguing that it was outmoded technology. In terms of A380 versus the 747X Boeing clearly lost the argument; the cheap and convenient solution was simply not effective. The indications today are that Boeing has been surprised, if not disappointed, in the sales and options taken out by the airlines on the A380, currently around 140 units.

The Sonic Cruiser

Continuing with its faith in the market forecast for higher speeds and lower sector times (through direct point-to-point operations), Boeing announced the Sonic Cruiser concept in 2001. The company had been working on this concept since 1999, as a high-speed replacement for the 767/A300. This would still leave the market open for the 747 and 777 to compete for the remaining longer range, high-density, hub-to-hub operations. There is evidence that Boeing even conducted SST studies around this time, so convinced was it that speed would become a dominant factor in future markets. However, supersonic transport studies were once again abandoned on the grounds of environmental concerns in favour of the high-speed subsonic Sonic Cruiser. Boeing believed that cruising at around Mach 0.98, in the so called 'sweet spot' of the cruise drag curve, it could achieve a 20% improvement in cruise speed over current subsonic jets, with relatively little increase in fuel burn. In the event, the Sonic Cruiser proved to be another 'blind alley' for Boeing. As many had predicted from the start, although cruise speed was increased significantly, there was only a marginal potential reduction in sector times offered by cruising at transonic/near supersonic speeds and this held relatively little appeal when set against the elevated fuel burn and environmental noise impact.

The 787

Late in 2002, the Sonic Cruiser was finally 'laid to rest', (*Flight International,* 9 December 2003, p. 25*)*. In its place came the Boeing 7E7 – a proposal for a super efficient transport aimed at realizing Boeing's fixation with direct point-to-point commercial operations, with greatly reduced direct operating costs. With the launch and abandonment of two major projects in short order since the turn of the millennium, Boeing's credibility now depended critically on the daunting prospect of realizing the promise of the 7E7.

A board decision on the Boeing 7E7 was announced at the end of 2003, but some further time was then required to resolve technical risks, particularly with engine selection, while the aircraft derivatives were still under review. However, as an illustration of Boeing's change of tack and its new emphasis on technological advancement, the company has proposed that the airframe will comprise some 50% composite materials with large monolithic parts manufactured from composites.

The full industrial launch of the 7E7 occurred in May 2004 (the 7E7 formally became the 787 in January 2005) when Boeing received an order for 50 of the new aircraft from Japan's All Nippon Airways, (*Flight International,* 4-10 May 2004). The launch, and the order, showed the benefits to Boeing from the US's strong political relationship with Japan. Indeed, the order appeared little more than an offset arrangement; a bargain struck in return for giving Japan a major chunk of the program. The aerospace trade press were quick to see the underlying logic. As *Flight International* noted:

> Japan has played a pivotal role in getting the 7E7 programme off the ground, and formal launch will lead to final approval by the Japanese government of a loan scheme to help local manufacturers cover their 7E7 development costs. The government has held off approving the loans pending a launch order and a master programme contract between Boeing and its three major Japanese suppliers, (*Flight International,* 4-10 May 2004, p. 8).

Increased International Offsets and Component Sourcing

The US aerospace industry, and Boeing in particular, was the single largest contributor to the US manufactured export trade over many years up to the 1990s (Patillo, 1998). The industry was built on the back of US developments of bombers and fighters for the Second World War, during which time the US built over 300,000 aircraft to support the war effort (Patillo, 2000). As a result, as we showed in Chapter 2, Boeing, and US commercial aerospace in general, owes much of its success to technology developed via US government funding. But now the US aerospace industry is in decline and has been so for the last two decades.

This decline has accelerated in recent years, in large part due to the development and competition from aerospace industries in the emerging industrial economies of the Far East, as well as the growth and competition from Airbus in Europe. Buyers of commercial aircraft around the world and their governments have imposed purchasing conditions on Boeing that have led to the overseas transfer of aircraft design and manufacturing, (MacPherson and Pritchard, 2004, p. 4). International offset agreements and component sourcing has become a major feature of Boeing programs over the recent past. While this has sustained market share for Boeing in some regions (the Far East in particular) in the short and medium term, it has come at a price for US aerospace employment. In 2003 the US aerospace industry had its lowest level of employment since the Second World War, with 12% of the workforce having been laid off since the attacks of 11 September 2001, (AIA, 2003). It does not bode well for the future of Boeing, as these emerging aerospace industries develop technological capabilities to equal if not surpass those of Boeing, all achieved with considerably lower labour costs.

The growth in capability of Boeing's industrial partners in Asia represents a dilemma with collaboration that has been highlighted by MIT's Jonathan Tucker. In his 'partners and rivals' model of collaboration, Tucker showed how larger companies receive a welfare benefit from collaboration, but simultaneously experience a positional loss in industrial ranking, as their technical capability flows across to their partner, (Tucker, 1991, pp. 83-86). Thus in the long term the kind of partnership Boeing has engaged in with Japan was bound to erode Boeing's relative position in world aerospace.

As well as declining employment, the intellectual power of the US industry is also being reduced. As figure 6.2 below shows, in 1986 the US aerospace industry had more than 140,000 scientists working in R&D, but in 2003 the figure was just 24,000, (AIA, 2003). This fits with the picture presented above of the overall declining attractiveness of the US industry for graduate engineering employment highlighted by the Aerospace Industry Association. Exporting capability abroad is not a good way to entice in a future generation of employees.

Asia's Growing Capability

The aerospace industries in Japan, China and South Korea are developing rapidly and investment in new technologies, tooling and facilities is moving apace. Japanese SST research contributed much knowledge to the ill-fated Sonic Cruiser program and Boeing is already much indebted to Japanese industry and research laboratories for advanced materials and systems developments to support current and future programs. On the 787, Boeing has given 35% of the airframe workshare to the Japanese while overall, as Figure 6.3 below indicates, about 65% will be manufactured overseas.

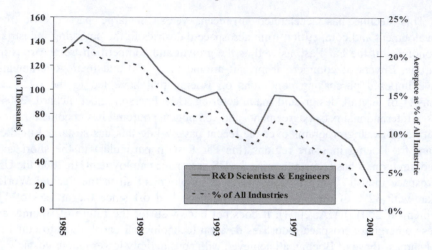

Figure 6.2   US Aerospace Scientists and Engineers Working in R&D
Credit: US AIA 2003.

Boeing's 787 program is also receiving about US$1.4 billion of Japanese government subsidy, as well as US$500m from Italy, quite ironic given the company's recent complaints about the identical European supports, (*The Economist*, 29 November 2003, p. 86). It would seem that under certain circumstances Boeing is comfortable with direct subsidies for aircraft manufacture, given the way that its strategic partners in Japan are funding their share of the development of the 787. Japanese partners Kawasaki Heavy Industries, Mitsubishi Heavy Industries and Fujitsu Heavy Industries are to receive non-repayable grants from the Japanese government's Ministry of Economy, Trade and Industry (METI) worth about US$500m. In addition other low-interest repayable loans will come from the Development Bank of Japan. These will be worth about US$959m, with some elements not even repayable. In total this could be close to 75% of the Japanese development bill for their 35% share of the 787.

With high labour costs in Japan this offset move makes little sense from a purely commercial point of view. What must be the real driver is the political relationship as the platform for Japanese sales, plus the development subsidy to attenuate risk. But as MacPherson and Pritchard observe the price is a transfer of whole aircraft manufacturing capability to Japan: '… the transfer of wing manufacturing and assembly expertise to Japanese companies effectively gives Japan 'total production competence' with regard to commercial airframes', (MacPherson and Pritchard, 2004, p. 30).

7E7 Structures Work Share

■	Boeing	35%
■	Japan	35%
▨	Vought/Alenia	26%
■	Other	4%

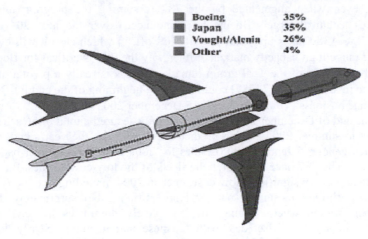

Figure 6.3　　787 Airframe Workshare
Credit: Boeing.

Conclusion: the Current Outlook

Boeing forecasts for aircraft sales over the next 20 years are not very different to those of Airbus in terms of aircraft numbers. (Airbus, *Global Market Forecast, 2002,* http://www.airbus.com/pdf/media/GMF2002_full_issue.pdf) Both postulate a virtual doubling in the world fleet of commercial jets by 2022. However, the forecast mix of aircraft types and sizes differs significantly between the two companies. Boeing, sticking to its forecasts of the last five years and more, seems to be of the conviction that more frequent and direct services will reduce the demand for very large aircraft and that the longer-range market will be dominated by intermediate-sized aircraft; sales of very large jets will decline commensurately.[1] Regional aircraft sales will see significant growth. In contrast, Airbus, investing in and developing the A380, still sees a strong and growing market for very large aircraft.

Either way, Boeing is not well placed to exploit this expanding market. It has only two products (the 777 and NG 737 derivatives) currently in production, that have a reasonable product life cycle remaining and capable of meeting the exacting

---

[1] These Boeing forecasts have appeared in the wake of the airlines rejecting the various 747 derivatives that were offered to customers in the 1990s.

standards of 21st century commercial air travel and airline economic operations. Even then, the Next-Generation 737 derivatives are based on a 1960s design. It remains to be seen whether Boeing can compete across the market with these aircraft, even when augmented by the 787 (assuming the program meets the ambitious technical targets Boeing has announced) over the next 20 years, or whether the A380 takes up where the 747 left off, in which case it will dominate the long range/high capacity market. Either way the 787 is critical for Boeing, as Richard Aboulafia of the Teal group remarked, 'This is really a pivotal moment. Failure to invest in the 7E7 [787] could mean the beginning of the end for Boeing's … airplane business', (*Business Week*, 15 December 2003).

At the end of December 2004 Boeing had only secured a total of 56 sales of the 787. Yet in summer 2004 Boeing predicted 200 sales by the year's end, (*Seattle Post Intelligencer*, 5 January 2005). Sales for 2004 also showed other bad omens for Boeing. The 737 once dominated the fleets of the low-cost airlines. But Airbus won virtually every significant low-cost order in 2004, including one for 70 planes from Air-Berlin and its start-up partner, Niki Luftfahrt. Not surprisingly, the only geographic region where Boeing still completely dominates the civil aircraft market is Japan. The offset deal with Japanese manufacturers clearly does pay dividends at the political and sales level. Boeing is seemingly aware of the crisis in its sales performance. In 2004, CEO Harry Stonecipher replaced sales boss Toby Bright with Scott Carson, the chief of the Connexion in-flight internet business. However, the analysis presented here suggests that the problem is the product not the sales pitch.

Chapter 7

Interlude: The Airbus vs. Boeing Trans-Atlantic Trade and Subsidy Battle

Introduction

The strategic character of the aeronautics industry makes it of key importance to governments. Therefore, not surprisingly, the great contest between Boeing and its European rival, Airbus, has been played out on the political stage as well as in the commercial and technological arena. Since the 1980s trade friction and even outright conflict has occurred between Europe and the US over Airbus. This chapter investigates aspects of the trade dispute over Airbus, which at the time of writing in 2005 has led both parties to bring WTO actions. The analysis here challenges the engrained assumption that it is only the European side that has received state support. In order to put the issue in historical and theoretical context some simplified aspects of trade theory are discussed below.

Basic Elements of Trade Theory

According to the now-dominant neo-classical (liberal) school of economics the ideal structure for world trade is one based on open and free markets. Free trade is based on the efficiency maximising principle of comparative advantage. The logic of comparative advantage is disarmingly simple: a country should produce and export goods which it can manufacture more efficiently than its trading rivals; alternatively it should import goods produced with greater efficiency by other countries. From a liberal point of view the aim is to secure an international division of labour based on economic efficiency. Because of factor endowments in capital, labour and land, particular countries will have a 'natural' advantage in some economic sectors which they should exploit.

The theory of comparative advantage, developed by liberals such as Ricardo, Smith, and J. S. Mill, undoubtedly captures an abstract principle of economic efficiency. However, when the theory collides with the real world significant problems emerge with its application. National economies exist within the boundaries of nation states which have their own economic agendas. In modern industrial societies governments have been acutely conscious of a strategic hierarchy of industries which are ranked in terms of factors, such as: degree of value added by labour, international prestige and contribution to national security.

In particular, states have been anxious not to be wholly dependent on trading partners for industrial technology they regard as critical to their science/technology base and national security. Aerospace is a classical example of this principle. In the real world nations have pursued strategies to catch-up and overtake other countries in critical industrial technologies, such as aerospace and defense. This is why the states of East Asia are putting so much effort into building space and aeronautics sectors today.

So-called 'welfare' economists have attacked the policy of government industrial support as leading to distortions and inefficiencies, but this is whistling in the wind. Seen from a mercantilist political economy perspective industrial policy strategies to bolster and support certain industrial sectors make eminent sense. Empirically, world trade follows much more a drive to secure competitive advantage rather than comparative advantage. The point is that through the use of certain policy instruments the framework of relative advantage in industrial trade can be altered through conscious government and corporate policy. Moreover, governments have a political responsibility to their citizens working in industrial sectors which are subject to foreign competition. They are required to lay down a framework for the economy which strengthens the overall competitive position of the nation. But perhaps more importantly, the technological capabilities embodied in aerospace are critical for defense and national security. As recent conflicts illustrate no state can be entirely secure today if it lacks airpower capability.

The reality of strategic trade, as opposed to free trade, is now widely recognized, but still hotly contested. After the successful catch-up strategy of Japan in consumer electronics and autos, inspired by the activities of the Ministry for International Trade and Industry (MITI, renamed METI in 2001), economists began to see the advantages which could accrue from effective industrial and trade policy. Balaam and Veseth put it neatly; 'The point is that in a more competitive environment, comparative advantages are no longer fixed but can be manufactured by states and firms', (1996, p. 23). Thus, rather than accept an accidental distribution of productive advantage, states have sought to improve their capability in high-technology/high value-added industries such as aerospace. As the perception of the role of strategic trade grew clearer the world's leading industrial nations became entangled in a series of bilateral and multilateral negotiations and disputes over how to secure 'fair play' in international trade; 'fair trade' replaced 'free trade' as the dominant normative principle.

In January 1995 these negotiations culminated in the creation of the World Trade Organisation (WTO), which now has global judicial authority over its members' trade. Structurally and ideologically these negotiations have been shaped by the US pressing Japan and later the European Union (EU) over trade issues. However, as the case of aeronautics illustrates, the issue of a level playing field for trade is extremely complex. What needs to be understood is that free-market dogma is itself a resource in the propaganda battle over trade issues. The United States, which has initiated much of the process of negotiation and organized most of the relevant international machinery, perceives itself to be the bastion of free trade. Yet the US has suffered a number of high profile reverses in the WTO arena. These WTO defeats seem to have caused much surprise in the US. However, in the view provided here, the real problem is that the US has been relatively unconscious of the role of its own government in supporting strategic industries. Former Secretary of Labor Robert Reich clearly grasps the point about supporting US firms: 'In return for prosperity, American society accepted the legitimacy and permanence of the core American Corporation. American officials took as one of their primary responsibilities the continued profitability of [these] corporations', (Reich, 1991, p. 58).

Anxiety over Airbus

As we have seen, Airbus's growth and steady success, ultimately leading to a 50% market share, has been anathema to many in the United States. With all the advantages of scale and scope economies and the historically accumulated competence in the workforce, plus huge defense contracts, the leading position of the US aerospace firms must have appeared secure. Thus Airbus's rise has been a profound and unwelcome shock. In the circumstances it is perhaps not surprising that the leading US aeronautics firms have tended to explain Airbus's achievements as resulting from unfair business practices and, in particular, the advantages gained from European government subsidies. In consequence a key dimension of the Airbus/Boeing competition has existed in the highly politicized world of diplomatic exchanges over the aircraft trade issue. In essence, when the US side has perceived Airbus to be moving forward in the market it has cried foul and frequently threatened, but rarely taken, GATT or WTO legal action.

Free Trade as a Political Ideology

Political ideology is embodied in beliefs and values which express the interests of individuals, groups and nations. It expresses philosophical ideas but is also linked to achieving political ends. Ideology also represents political belief systems which give human life meaning and allow individuals to share a common view of their social and political experience. In the US a core element in the dominant political ideology is economic liberalism, which enshrines principles of free trade and *laissez-faire*. State interference in the economy is regarded as illegitimate.

According to orthodox liberal scholarship the United States assumed the role of global hegemonic power after 1945, with a mission to spread the creed of free trade. As Krugman and Obstfeld note, 'Since World War II the United States has advocated free trade in the world economy, viewing international trade as a force not only for prosperity but also for world peace', (Krugman and Obstfeld, 1994. p. 5). In consequence of this understanding it has been widely assumed that after 1945 US leaders sought to use their hegemonic power to institute a global regime of free trade based on the principles of neo-classical and Keynesian economics.

This was the burden of the Bretton Woods agreement of June 1944 and it informed the gradualist strategy adopted by the General Agreement on Tariffs and Trade (GATT) in 1947. This historically grounded assumption has been further embellished by mainstream liberal theories in International Political Economy, which have posited the model of hegemonic stability in the post-war period. In this model a stable and liberal economic order was made possible because of US global dominance and its willingness to tolerate the costs of global leadership, (Stein, 1984, p. 355).

Hegemonic Stability and Free Trade

With regard to the post-1945 era the liberal theory of hegemonic stability conceives the structural characteristics of the global economy of the period as determined by the unparalleled power and resources of the United States. In particular the hegemon is seen as providing a series of public goods - peace, free trade and sound international finance - which are essential to the system. From a liberal viewpoint the hegemon has an essentially benevolent motivation for bearing the costs of the system. Although it is conceded that the hegemonic power also has much to gain. The system, then, results from enlightened self interest and in trade terms is a positive-sum game i.e. all parties can benefit.

While we believe that the liberal model has some descriptive utility, we argue here that its uncritical application overstates the real commitment of the US to free markets and free trade. In essence the theory takes the value system which underwrites the liberal international economic order as being derived from the dominant US model of economics; the self-evident US commitment to liberalism. But the model presumes that the actual empirical economy of the hegemonic state corresponds fairly closely to a *laissez-faire* framework. Alternatively, we see the issue of hegemony from a realist perspective. In our view the post-1945 move to a liberal economic order resulted, at least in part, from the push of American self-interest. Open markets obviously suit the nation-state with the strongest industries. But more significantly if a hegemonic state seeks to foster free trade amongst its trading rivals, yet manages to protect some of its own key industries, it will always emerge the winner in a zero-sum game. In the particular case of civil aerospace, which we focus on here, the strength of the US's industry can be seen as the result of public support and industrial policy. In the American aerospace industry we have an example which contradicts key liberal assumptions about the *laissez-faire* nature of the US economy.

We take issue with the simplistic liberal model of the US economy. In particular we challenge the idea that all sectors of the US economy have corresponded in any straightforward way to a *laissez-faire* model. In the authors' view this lack of fit between the model and empirical reality results from political ideology and culture. The philosophy of economic liberalism has been and continues to be a cornerstone of American political identity. But particularly in the US the ideological and discursive practices of liberalism simply ignore aspects of social reality that contradict key liberal assumptions regarding the organisation of state, economy and society. In this case the features of US economic history and current practice which would challenge the plausibility of a liberal model. More broadly it can be argued that the liberal model of the state – qua minimalism – has not been able to accommodate several historically evolving features of the US political structure. These include:

> The state's early role in capital accumulation, e.g. giving private companies land for railway construction (In Minnesota and Washington 25% of state land was given away to private interests);

> The advocacy of mercantilism by leading federalist politicians such as Hamilton;

> The state's advocacy of high tariffs during the 19th century to protect infant industries;

> The state's function in the National Recovery Administration and the New Deal;

> The state's security role in the Second World War and its assumption of permanent post-1945 responsibility for global security, (Wolfe, 1977, ch.1).

With regard to our analysis here concerning the commercial aircraft industry this last point is really the key one. In the post-1945 era the US state has had, in effect, a covert industrial policy for the aerospace and defense sector, which has been every bit as effective and real as the more overt policies of its European allies. The policy was funded by the Pentagon, its aim derived from security strategy, its beneficiaries the large manufacturers of defense and related equipment and its consequence the maintenance of huge corporations in high technology sectors, such as aerospace. But, of course, as we have argued, this does not fit easily with the engrained American free market self image. Leading US post-war economist, John Kenneth Galbraith, captures the irony implicit in this:

> Only someone with an instinct for inconvenience suggests that firms such as Lockheed or General Dynamics, which do most of their business with the government, make extensive use of plants owned by government, have their working capital supplied by the government, have their cost overruns socialised by government … are anything but the purest manifestations of private enterprise, (Galbraith, 1973, pp. 3-4).

The Real US Policy

In the post-1945 era in the Anglo-Saxon world the philosophy and language of mercantilism has been pushed to one side by the ideology and rhetoric of liberalism. But in our view the dominant liberal characterization of the US economy in the post-war period is exaggerated and overblown. Some sectors, such as consumer electronics, have felt the chill wind of global competition but others have not. Protection has been apparent in agriculture at one extreme and aerospace at the other. Judith Goldstein has outlined three models of trade relations based on an analysis of ideological and institutional factors, which determine the prospects for political support. She conceives fair trade and redistributive trade as additional models to the orthodox free trade mantra, (Goldstein, 1988, p. 216).

But based on our realist perspective we would add a fourth category of strategic trade in products centrally linked to issues of national security. Post-1945 US trade in defense and aerospace has never simply been about commercial factors. Civil aeronautics exports have been closely linked to security issues and on occasion have arisen on the back of defense sales. A vital aspect of American success in exporting civil aircraft has been the USA's role as a provider of security to friendly countries. As Anthony Sampson comments, 'the Pentagon has been relentless in making the connection between the commercial and diplomatic choices', (Sampson, 1977, p. 269). In terms of assessing which industries are likely to receive aid and protection, Goldstein noted how those prone to unemployment and those considered successful and highly competitive were most likely to obtain high-level political assistance. Again aerospace fits this categorization.

The more overt aerospace industrial policy of the Clinton-era was related precisely to the competitive challenge mounted by Europe in civil aeronautics in the 1980s and 1990s and the high levels of unemployment experienced in the US industry after the end of the Cold War. According to Jens Van Scherpenberg the neo-mercantilist aspects of this process became more pronounced as the constraints on conflict with allies in Europe were loosened. As Van Scherpenberg noted, 'Linking military dominance with an aggressive pursuit of economic interests has since become a core element of the US economic policy agenda, (Van Scherpenberg, 1997, p. 107).

The Airbus-Boeing Dispute

As we saw in Chapter 4, in order to meet the huge costs of aircraft development the Airbus partner companies agreed loans with their governments known as launch aid. Such aid was a strategic commitment by the Airbus governments to the new collaborative venture formed in 1970. But these loans have become highly contentious elements in the conflict which materialized between the EU and US over allegations of unfair competition.

Even in the early days when Airbus had a small toehold in the market it was beginning to attract political attention from the US. It was clear that the US manufacturers were starting to use their political muscle to try and emasculate Airbus, as a sale of two A300s to TransBrasil in 1975 was lost due to interference from Washington, which denied the Brazilians the finance, (Lynn, 1995, p. 117).

The strategic nature of trade and manufacture in large commercial aircraft was also evident even as early as the late 1970s, when Airbus was aiming to develop its second product, the A310. Concurrently, the British government was seeking to merge the UK's two largest aerospace companies, the British Aircraft Corporation (BAC) and Hawker Siddeley Aviation (HSA). They were also reconsidering the decision to remain outside the Airbus consortium. As the newly created British national champion emerged - British Aerospace (BAe) - it was clear that its participation in Airbus would be welcomed in Europe. It was also clear that the new aircraft would require a different wing to the A300B, which British expertise could provide. Across the Atlantic, Boeing saw a tactical opportunity. Now to some degree sensitized to the potential of Airbus, after the sale to Eastern Airlines, Boeing moved to recruit BAe as a major subcontractor on its rival to the A310, the 757. Boeing's aim was to '... prevent the return of the British to Airbus and draw in the British airframer and engine builder in constructing the 757', (Picq, 1990, pp. 116-117). In general, this was a none-too-subtle move to tie-up British engineering expertise and capital and keep the UK estranged from Airbus. But the tactic failed and British Aerospace joined the Airbus consortium on the A310 project with a 20% workshare, (Thornton, 1995, p. 104).

The incident described above, which involved contacts at Head of State level, emphasizes and illustrates the high-level strategic competition in the sphere of aircraft trade and manufacture. But this was just a foretaste of what would become an intense and acrimonious rivalry. In the late 1970s orders for Airbus's new aircraft signalled the start of a global sales competition with Boeing and McDonnell Douglas (MDC), which became increasingly bitter. By 1979/80 Airbus was taking a 20% share of the market for large commercial aircraft and US manufacturer Lockheed decided to abandon the airliner business. Airbus also showed that it could outgun the Americans in the area of technical innovation. On the A300B the technology was not particularly innovative but the overall concept was. On the A310, though, Airbus pioneered significant technical innovations, such as the FFCC (Forward Facing Crew Cockpit), wingtip fences and a rear fuel tank in the horizontal tail plane in order that fuel could be moved to reconfigure the aircraft's centre of gravity, allowing improved trim and fuel consumption. In Seattle and Long Beach some of these innovations were met with scepticism, but they are now industry standards, as is Airbus's innovative vertical acceleration instrumentation.

With a furious sales battle going on in sectors such as the Middle East, US industry chiefs began to take their concerns about Airbus to the federal government. On the US side a concerted diplomatic effort was made to prevent the development of Airbus's third product, the single aisle, twin-engine A320. The politics of this bear consideration.

Anti-Airbus Diplomacy

In order to develop the A320 Airbus began looking for finance and potential customers in new environments. One approach was made to the Canadians through the government of the province of Quebec, as Airbus was hoping to secure Canadian industrial participation. But although not public knowledge, the US political authorities had been shadowing Airbus activity for some time. When the Canadian initiative came to light, the United States Trade Representative (USTR), William E. Brock, sent a letter to the Canadian Minister of Industry, Trade and Commerce. The letter had a tone that was clearly threatening, 'Any implied or actual commitment on the part of Canada to purchase Airbus products or encourage their purchase, as an adjunct to industrial participation, would be a major concern to the United States Government', (Quoted McIntyre, 1992, p. 162). Ironically, USTR Brock justified his intervention on the grounds that Airbus Industrie (AI) was using government-to-government politics to secure project funding and sales. Clearly, using the same methods to block a project launch was seen in a different light.

As the decade wore on, the US side increased the pressure on Europe through the lobbying of its USTRs and other diplomatic channels. But it became clear that the A320 would go ahead and American anxiety grew. In the market place, blocking tactics failed as the DC-9 derivative, the MD-80, and Boeing's 737-300 failed to blunt the attraction of the new Airbus. As we have seen, after its launch in 1987 the A320 became the fastest selling commercial aircraft in history. In the US Boeing executives wanted a Cabinet task force to monitor Airbus and to co-ordinate export support in the United States. At the roll out of the 767-300 in Seattle in 1985, Boeing's Tom Bacher asserted that the company was, '… getting pretty damn mad', (McIntyre, p. 167).

This comment of Bacher's gives us a clue as to the cause of the bitterness that had been widely expressed in the US concerning Airbus. When the consortium started manufacturing aircraft no one across the Atlantic was taking it that seriously. But as it began to eat into US market share, a sense of unease was apparent and a feeling was occasionally manifested that predominance in aeronautics was almost an American right. In consequence the assumption has been that Airbus's success must, by definition, represent some form of sharp or dubious practice. Thus, as the industry dragged government into the dispute, a certain ideological zeal was apparent. But what has never really been evident is recognition that Airbus was doing the right things and actually satisfying its customers.

Turning the Heat Up

The transatlantic war of words over subsidy intensified during the years 1985-1988. This was because the US side had failed to block the launch of the A320 and was now alarmed by both the scale of A320's sales and the launch of the new A330/340. US policy now became clear. First, intensified use of the GATT subsidy rules on a multilateral front, and secondly, bilateral negotiations with individual Airbus governments. The second tactic was designed to open up splits amongst the Airbus partners.

Negotiations began in 1986 after a French government offer to discuss US concerns over sales inducements. However, the United States Trade Representative

(USTR) wanted a much wider discussion to include 'government subsidies to Airbus' and orders of Airbus aircraft by 'state-owned European airlines', (McGuire, 1997, p. 122). As the tension grew in the mid-1980s USTRs began to lobby European ministers directly on the Airbus issue. As McIntyre asserts, the American side began to believe they were making some progress with their continuing call for the industry in Europe to be run on stricter commercial lines. (1992, p. 173). In order to increase the pressure in 1987 the US called for ministerial talks, with the target now clearly the blocking of the launch of the new long-range A330/340. The US position was blunt and hard-line, ' ... the US government was not going to stand idly by and accept the unfettered subsidisation of Airbus, particularly when that unfettered subsidisation was leading to displacement of US exports by the number one export manufacturing industry in the United States', (McIntyre, 1992, p. 176).

The tough line was echoed by Boeing, which began to crystallize its critique of Airbus's defects. In essence the US side began a process to try and undermine the Airbus consortium's credibility as a commercial organization and viable business. Using the assumptions of market economics and the legal framework of GATT, the US policy was aimed to delegitimate Airbus through accusations such as the following from the Department of Commerce: 'These subsidies lead to launch of new programs without viability, incorporation of technologies that cannot pay for themselves, building of whitetails that are offered at fire-sale prices and widespread underpricing to gain market share', (Quoted McIntyre, p. 176).

These comments are understandable but unjustifiable. In the 1970s, when the A300B came onto the market, new aircraft were stacking up on the tarmac and customers were in short supply. Further, no one in Europe was denying the role of state aid in Airbus's product development. But on the US side there was a continuing blindness to the role that defense procurement, tax breaks and publicly-funded NASA and DoD R&D played in the success of the American companies. Also, by the 1980s, the stereotypical American view of Airbus was outmoded. Airlines, including US ones, were buying the product because it met their requirements. Moreover, the European consortium's investment in high technology was reaping dividends in the growing perception in the marketplace that Airbus had some competitive advantages. Thus, in the early 1990s, it is not surprising that Bill Clinton's economic advisor, Laura Tyson, noted how Airbus had 'achieved technological parity with Boeing ... ' (Tyson, 1992, p. 155).

Aide Memoir: European Capability

The attitudes expressed in the US about Airbus were historically misinformed. In reality Airbus was just capitalizing on an older but previously unfulfilled European capability in aeronautics. At times some of Boeing's claims about Airbus would even imply that Europe should have remained outside of the large commercial aircraft business altogether. In 1985 Boeing's Tom Bacher suggested that Europe should stick to producing trains, (McIntyre, 1992, p. 167). But this rests on a rather self-serving US amnesia regarding aeronautics history. As the Senate Armed Services Committee noted in 1997:

> Please remember that the United States did not build the first high performance fighters or the first jet engine or the first ballistic rocket or the first commercial jet aircraft. However, over the last 80 years whenever the federal government stepped up and established a national priority supported by adequate funding, we moved forward to achieve dominance, (Senate Armed Services Committee: Subcommittee on Acquisition and Technology, 10 April, 1997).

In fact, former Boeing CEO Phil Condit had a more accurate grasp of the facts than his colleague Tom Bacher:

> There's one thing about Boeing you have to remember … We haven't been first very often … The first jet transport was the British Comet. The first trijet was the [British] Trident; only about a hundred were built, while we sold more than eighteen hundred 727s. The first twinjet was the Caravelle, the second was the BAC One-Eleven, the third was the DC-9, and we were fourth with the 737, which outsold them all. People worry about Boeing being late but being late has given us a chance to really gauge what the customer wants, and make sure we're meeting it, (Quoted, Sterling, 1992, p. 458).

As Condit implies, in the past Europe had often been the leader but had failed in sales and marketing and not given the customer what they wanted. Thus, in reality, Europe's 1980s renaissance in aeronautics meant that a traditional capability, which expressed itself historically in often being first, was coupled, in the form of Airbus, with more credible business performance and market appraisal. In the US the nemesis of the number two and three players, McDonnell Douglas and Lockheed, was blamed on Airbus and the subsidy factor. But their failure was entirely the result of self-inflicted wounds and an inability to please their customers.

The Battle of the Reports and the 1992 Agreement

US accusations of unwarranted subsidy were taken around European capitals in the late 1980s in an attempt to blunt the A330/340 program. Ultimately, though the issue was to end up under the jurisdiction of the GATT Subsidies Committee.

As large civil aircraft and engines are sold with a US dollar ticket, non-American producers are vulnerable to falls in the US dollar exchange rate. In the 1980s, mindful of this vulnerability and also short of cash, Deutsche Airbus began to negotiate an exchange rate protection scheme with the German government. In the meantime negotiations were also in place to sell off the Deutsche Airbus parent company Messerschmitt-Bolkow-Blohm (MBB) to Daimler Benz. The foreign exchange (FOREX) rate scheme therefore became tied up with the wider process of restructuring the German aerospace industry. The FOREX scheme to support sales of A320 and A330/340 was approved by the German government in 1988 and the CEC in 1989. This FOREX deal was worth DM2.6 billion. From the US point of view this was the straw that broke the camel's back. The issue was taken to GATT.

The US promptly began action under the GATT Subsidies code. Arguably, the German FOREX scheme was a subsidy too far and, in the opinion of many commentators, not carefully enough crafted to avoid US attention. It clearly violated the explicit GATT prohibition on export subsidies. The US won its case before the GATT Subsidies Dispute Panel in January 1992.

Gellman

Prior to this GATT case the US Department of Commerce had commissioned a report into Airbus's funding by Gellman Research Associates, of Jenkintown, Pennsylvania. The report, *An Economic and Financial Review of Airbus Industrie*, issued in September 1990, was meant as a damning indictment of Airbus's financial arrangements. The brief had been to, 'deepen the understanding of the complex web of relations between the participating companies, the governments and the AI [Airbus Industrie] consortium', (Thornton, 1995, p. 138). However, the report was in reality much narrower and dealt exclusively with the question of Airbus's credentials as a commercial organization.

The report focused upon the economics of Airbus Industrie's civil aircraft programs and examined the potential effects of Airbus Industrie's activities on both the market for civil transport aircraft and on competing US firms. The Gellman team made clear from the outset that one of the primary reasons for undertaking the study was to compile and assess data and information on the Airbus Industrie operation and the levels of government support that its programs received. Furthermore, the Gellman team were tasked with clarifying 'the complex web of relations between the participating companies, the governments and the AI consortium', (Gellman, ES1). At the outset, however, Gellman emphasized the existence of 'a degree of uncertainty in the numeric estimates presented', (1990, ES1). This was appropriate as their calculations were necessarily based upon speculative price, quantity and cost estimates for past, current and future Airbus Industrie aircraft sales.

Using 1990-dollar values the Gellman Report claimed that Airbus had been the recipient of more than US$13 billion of government support since its inception in the late 1960s and that the real commercial market value of this subsidy was US$26 billion. The report's conclusions were highly critical and indicated that Airbus had distorted the US industry because of its state subsidy and ability to pursue ventures without regard to commercial criteria. In a wider context this pattern of thinking then became reinforced as scores of economists jumped on the anti-Airbus bandwagon. US textbooks on International Economics frequently cited

Airbus as a clear example of the damaging effects of industrial policy and strategic trade, (See Krugman and Obstfeld, 1994, pp. 278-286).

The Gellman team drew a number of important, although contentious, conclusions from their research and, in presenting an essentially negative view of the market role and performance of Airbus Industrie, made necessary a powerful response from the European consortium and effectively acted as the catalyst for the trade friction which has followed.

Arnold and Porter

Following Gellman's direct and uncompromising attack on the economic and commercial viability of the European aircraft industry, it was imperative that Europe produced a cogently argued response. The Arnold and Porter report, *US Government Support of the US Commercial Aircraft Industry*, was prepared by the Washington DC-based consultancy for the European Commission and issued in November 1991. It set out to undermine the conclusions of the Gellman report by offering a definitive picture of the significant degree of financial support historically and currently offered to US aircraft manufacturers by the US government and thereby challenging Gellman's 'privately-financed only' view of US industry. Arnold and Porter thus amplified the criticisms we have already outlined above.

The Arnold and Porter study was equally as direct as Gellman in the assertions it made about the US LCA industry and the support it receives from government, albeit in this case indirectly. Arnold and Porter's research identified 'massive systematic support to the US commercial aircraft industry pursuant to a long-standing US policy of striving to maintain US superiority in all areas of aeronautics technology', (1991, p. 1). In common with the Gellman report, Arnold and Porter draw attention to the lack of transparency in the data available upon which to base their research.

Despite the data problems identified, Arnold and Porter estimated that US government support to its own commercial aircraft industry in the period 1976 to 1991 was in the range of US$18 billion to US$22.05 billion. Using 1991 rather than historic prices to estimate the value of benefits accruing to the US aircraft industry from Department of Defense and NASA contracts, the estimated range of benefits amounted to between US$33.48 billion and US$41.49 billion.

Arnold and Porter identified three principal ways in which the US government supports the US commercial aircraft industry. First, substantial support for the aircraft industry in the US is received from US Department of Defense R&D budgets. Such was the over-riding strategic importance of the aeronautics industry to the US in the post-Second World War period that vast financial resources were dedicated to military aeronautics R&D. Since the key companies in the US commercial aircraft industry were engaged directly or indirectly in military aeronautics development and production, and that military and commercial aeronautics technology often overlap, it was inevitable that commercial aircraft development and production would derive very substantial crossover commercial benefits and synergy from their participation in military R&D.

Arnold and Porter cited what they termed 'quantum leaps' in US commercial aeronautics technology – the Boeing 707, the wide-body jets and the development of a supersonic civil transport plane – as examples of programs where substantial US government involvement was apparent in the period prior to each breakthrough, (1991, p. 2). They estimated that, since 1976, the US Department of Defense had spent some US$50 billion on aeronautics R&D, with at least US$6.34 billion reaching the two leading US aircraft producers of large commercial aircraft, Boeing and McDonnell Douglas, to finance aircraft-related R&D. Taking account of the proportion of these funds estimated to have been of benefit to the US LCA sector, Arnold and Porter suggested that it might have derived benefit amounting to between US$5.9 billion and US$9.7 billion of Department of Defense expenditure. In terms of 1991-dollar value (and accounting for opportunity costs and compound interest), this translates into commercial benefits measured in current prices of between US$12.42 billion and US$20.18 billion.

Arnold and Porter conceded the point that the Department of Defense did attempt to recapture a proportion of the private commercial benefits accruing to players in the US LCA industry from their involvement in military aeronautics R&D. However, they indicated that in the years between 1976 and 1990, less than US$200m had been recouped, representing a minuscule amount of the total funding committed. It should also be pointed out that DoD recoupment is no longer required from US firms.

The authors also emphasized that, as well as direct Defense Department R&D grants that flow to private US aircraft companies, the US also directly reimbursed these companies for in-house R&D projects that may have military application through the Independent Research and Development Program. Such is the current value of dual-use technologies in the aerospace industry that the commercial utility of such in-house, self-chosen research and development activity is even higher than in government-initiated R&D. In the decade and a half prior to the 1991 report, Arnold and Porter estimated that US aerospace companies had received about US$5 billion of such reimbursements from the US government, worth some US$1 billion to US$1.25 billion of likely benefit to the US commercial aircraft industry.

The second institutional locus of support identified by Arnold and Porter drew attention to US government subsidy for the US commercial aircraft industry, which emanated from NASA budgets. As one of its primary mission objectives, NASA is tasked with the promotion of US technological superiority in the aeronautics sector and therefore provides substantial funding for civil as well as military aeronautics R&D. Arnold and Porter estimated that, between 1976 and 1991, NASA has committed about US$8.9 billion to civil and military aeronautics R&D in the US. Much of this expenditure funded large-scale R&D projects of significant value to US civil aircraft manufacturers, for example the Aircraft Energy Efficient Program and the development of the supercritical wing. In addition, NASA provided funding for a whole range of smaller projects that focused on the encouragement of specific technological developments in aeronautics.

Taking NASA's role in supporting technological progress in US commercial aeronautics and the inter-linking of its civil and military R&D objectives together, Arnold and Porter estimated that some 90% of NASA R&D expenditure over the period since 1976, amounting to US$8 billion, represented a benefit to US commercial aeronautics. At current prices, they suggested that the value to the US commercial aircraft industry of this support would have been almost US$17 billion.

As well as assessing the contribution of NASA and the DoD to the US LCA sector, Arnold and Porter emphasized the specific ways in which the US tax system provided distinct benefits to the US civil aircraft industry. As they noted: 'The "completed contract method" for determining when contract income is subject to tax has allowed US aircraft manufacturers to reduce taxes by deferring substantial amounts of income. Use of domestic international sales corporations (DISCS) and foreign sales corporations (FSCS) also has permitted substantial deferrals', (1991, p. 5) The authors estimated that, over the 15 years to 1991, these important tax deferrals and exemptions benefited Boeing by approximately US$1.7 billion and McDonnell Douglas by some US$1.4 billion.

Overall, Arnold and Porter suggested that, far from the US civil aircraft industry being a privately funded operation with no government support, at least three identifiable and quantifiable major areas of support existed. The combined value of these government-funding mechanisms had, they asserted, provided the US industry with an estimated commercial benefit of between US$18 billion and US$22.5 billion between 1976 and 1991. In current 1991 prices, this support would have been valued at between US$33.48 billion and US$41.49 billion. On top of this massive government support for the domestic aircraft industry, the US government also provided various additional forms of aid including US aircraft manufacturers' use of government test facilities at reduced cost and occasional special purchases of aircraft by government (such as the KC-10s purchased by the US government from McDonnell Douglas in 1982).

Arnold and Porter concluded with the observation that, while exact measurement of US government support for its civil aircraft industry is impossible given the lack of transparency in available data, there was little doubt that such support had played a key role in securing and preserving the most important technological advances made by the US civil aircraft industry, helping to secure the position of the US commercial aircraft industry in increasingly competitive global markets.

In summary the Arnold and Porter study served to correct a number of biases and prejudices that previously informed the US view of EU/US trade in LCA. Chiefly Arnold and Porter demolished the myth that the US LCA industry was an entirely free enterprise operation divorced from the benefits of state support.

The Arnold and Porter study showed clearly that the US industry was embedded in an infrastructure for research and development, financing and commercial manufacturing assistance funded by the federal government, which greatly enhanced the competitiveness of American aerospace firms. As we have indicated above a key problem with this area of debate has been the presence of an *idée fix* in the US about the liberal nature of its economy and *laissez-faire*. Hence the conviction that there was no corporate welfare, no industrial policy and no support for strategic trade in aerospace products. Since the Arnold and Porter report that misconception, at least, has been less easy to sustain.

The 1992 Agreement

Although the US took the German FOREX Issue to the GATT Subsidies Panel, they were reluctant to bring a wider action against the EEC within the GATT framework. US trade officials feared that this would hamper progress in the new GATT Uruguay round. In addition, the US wanted to avoid the political consequences of a full-blown GATT dispute. The EEC also sought to keep the Airbus issue out of GATT, as the Europeans wanted to have the aircraft industry defined as a special case that was exempt from aspects of the wider subsidies code. Therefore a bilateral deal, outside the wider GATT framework, was attractive to both sides. In 1991 EEC/US negotiations continued on a back channel towards achieving a deal on European Airbus subsidies. Tacitly, European negotiators let the US side know that a reduction in launch aid supports for aircraft development might be acceptable. In return the US began to acknowledge the existence of indirect R&D supports and the possibility of placing a cap on this NASA/ DoD funding. In that respect Arnold and Porter had played a key role in reconfiguring the terms of the debate.

The EU and the US signed the *EU/US Bilateral Agreement on Trade in Large Civil Aircraft* in July 1992. On the European side, concessions ultimately reduced the permitted level of direct governmental support on aircraft programs down to 33% of program costs, subject to full repayment on a royalty basis over a term no longer than 17 years. Funding for Airbus aircraft development was also to be subjected to a 'critical project appraisal', to evaluate whether the program had a viable commercial basis. On the US side, it was conceded that indirect supports were significant in assisting the aerospace industry and, in similar fashion to direct subsidies, ought to be the subject of regulation. According to the 1992 Bilateral the annual value of such support should not exceed 3% of a nation's commercial aircraft industry's annual turnover or 4% of the annual civil turnover of any single firm in that nation's aircraft manufacturing industry. But a key weakness of the 1992 Bilateral for Europe has been the difficulty of monitoring compliance with the discipline on indirect supports. Although quantifying US R&D programs is relatively straightforward, determining precisely what is an indirect support to the US large commercial aircraft industry is much more problematic.

Renewed Hostility

In the early 1990s there seemed every chance of a trade war between the US and EU in commercial aeronautics. In the end, though, the 1992 Bilateral Agreement obviated this. But the 1992 Agreement did not end the tensions over EU/US trade in large commercial aircraft. Global recession and the end of the Cold War meant job losses and painful rationalization in the US Aerospace Industry. On the back of this, the Clinton Administration chose to reopen hostilities with a series of public statements about Airbus. After the July 1992 Bilateral Agreement, USTR Mickey Cantor referred to the EU side as 'screaming pigs stuck in a gate'. At the Everett Boeing plant in 1993 the President promised enhanced support for Boeing and blamed Airbus for US job losses. What was clear was that the new Democratic administration was going to pursue a more overt industrial policy, with strategies to bolster US high technology industries and a new brief for NASA to give its research more commercial relevance.

With regard to trade policy the Clinton era saw more pronounced state involvement in export advocacy and more unilateral interventions in global trade issues, such as the threat to impose penalties on firms trading with Cuba. Through the aegis of the Trade Promotion Co-ordinating Committee, the Departments of Commerce, Defense and State have been orchestrated a more overt neo-mercantilist policy, using executive level government actions in a global strategy to enhance export sales in high technology sectors. The late Secretary of Commerce, Ron Brown, was killed in the former Yugoslavia, while on just such a mission to secure US export sales.

Another example of increased sales advocacy was the 1993 Boeing Saudi deal, which involved Presidential contacts with King Fahd and other Saudi authorities and was announced to the world's media on the steps of the White House. This move should not have engendered surprise. President Clinton had been elected on a ticket to secure American jobs and improve living standards. His advisers also reinforced his mercantilist instincts. As Lynn notes, 'Around him were theorists and advisers who believed that it was time to start turning the military and political might of the United States into harder coinage: money, trade, jobs', (Lynn, 1997, p. 1) According to some commentators political involvement may even have gone further. Press reports asserted that agents of the National Security Agency bugged the Airbus sales team at the time of the Saudi deal, (*The Guardian*, 26 March 1997, p. 3).

The Legacy of the 1992 Agreement

As we have shown, an intractable problem in the early days of the exchanges over commercial aircraft trade was a reluctance on the US side to see any government funded contribution to the performance of American aerospace companies, because of a blanket assumption that the US did not operate industrial policies. However, the trade discussions of the last two decades and the proliferation of reports into government funding and supports have now created a dialogue where at least certain parameters are known. The 1992 Bilateral Agreement on Trade in Civil Aircraft formalized an acknowledgement that indirect support did exist in the US system. Nevertheless, the EU side was posed with a serious difficulty. The real value of indirect support to US manufacturers is inherently contestable in terms of the precise contribution to the commercial viability and competitiveness of products that reach the market place. Despite the July 1992 agreement members of the US administration continue to deny the contribution made by publicly funded R&D to the commercial aircraft industry. Moreover, the calculation of the worth of DoD and NASA programs that benefit US firms is also difficult because some figures are hidden in black, secret programs that are classified. For this reason, policing adherence to the 1992 agreement on the US side has been problematic.

The Seeds of the New Trade Conflict

The US civil aeronautics industry is one of the jewels in the American industrial crown. As Mowery and Rosenberg comment, 'Judged against almost any criterion of performance – growth in outputs, exports, productivity or innovation – the civilian aircraft industry must be considered a star performer in the [post-Second World War] US economy', (Quoted, Tyson, 1992, p. 155). In addition it is the largest exporter and a symbol of national prestige, which resonates with America's optimism about the role of technology in society. As a result it is not surprising that the continuing decline of the US's share of the world market in the 1990s has caused shock and dismay.

Because of its decline in market share Boeing received extensive support and subsidy from NASA in the 1990s to enable it to launch new products with which to compete against Airbus. Two of NASA's focused research programs (Advanced Subsonic Transport (AST) and High Speed Research (HSR) were geared to the prospective launch of new commercial aircraft; one a supersonic and the other a new subsonic aircraft. The subsidy is clear as NASA funded the research programs, which were done in partnership with Boeing engineers. At the conclusion of these programs the technology was then handed over to Boeing for use on future commercial products. As Table 7.1 reveals, nearly one billion dollars was spent on the 1990s AST program.

Table 7.1   **NASA Advanced Subsonic Transport Budget (US$m)**

FY93	FY94	FY95	FY96	FY97	FY98	FY99	Total
$12.4	$101.3	$150.1	$169.8	$173.6	$211.1	$89.6	$907.9

Source: NASA Budget, 1999.

The other focused program, the High Speed Research (HSR, see Table 7.2), received even greater funding, with one contract to Boeing worth US$440m. By 1999 nearly US$1.5 billion had been spent on the program. Boeing walked away from actually developing the planned supersonic transport, but the technology was applied to the Sonic Cruiser concept. This technology will also be present on the 787 and helps to explain why Boeing is so confident about the new technology. Figure 7.1 shows NASA technology incorporated into US aircraft.

Table 7.2   **NASA High Speed Research Budget (US$m)**

FY93	FY94	FY95	FY96	FY97	FY 98	FY99	Total
$117.0	$187.2	$221.3	$233.3	$243.1	$245.0	180.7	$1427.6

Table 7.3   **NASA Aeronautical Research & Technology Budget (US$m)**

	FY93	FY94	FY95	FY96	FY97	FY98	FY93-98
R&T Base	436.5	448.3	366.3	354.7	404.2	418.3	2428.3
AST	12.4	101.3	150.1	169.8	173.6	211.1	818.3
HSR	117.0	187.2	221.3	233.3	243.1	245.0	1246.9
Other	299.7	83.9	144.3	159.5	23.3	45.7	756.4
TOTAL	865.6	820.7	882.0	917.3	844.2	920.1	5249.9

Source: NASA.

Aircraft	NACA/NASA R&T Incorporated
Ford Tri-Motor	Wing contour and wing cowlings developed by NACA to improve airflow characteristics
Douglas DC-3	Low-drag engine cowling design developed by NACA
Lockheed Constellation	NACA's aerodynamic drag reduction experimental research results and the low-drag engine cowling
Boeing 747	NASA research in high-bypass jet engines, low drag nacelles, swept-wing, airfoils, noise reduction, transonic aerodynamics, and structural research
McDonnell Douglas MD-11	Winglet design, supercritical airfoils, digital electronic controls, numerous engine design improvements, high-lift systems, transonic aerodynamics and structural concepts
Boeing 777	Digital flight controls, glass cockpit, quiet engine nacelles, aerodynamic design codes, flight management systems, graphite-epoxy structures and transonic supercritical airfoils

Figure 7.1 NASA Technology Incorporated in US Aircraft
Adapted from NASA/DoD Aerospace Knowledge Diffusion Project, 1997, p. 37.

In the 1990s, NASA expenditure on aeronautics research and technology (Table 7.3) was huge and its purpose was to ensure continued US leadership in the sector.

Boeing has also benefited from the NASA Research and Technology Base Program. According to NASA's own budget statement the agency provided the following technology for US aircraft:

➢ Supercritical Wing for the 757 and 767;
➢ Winglets for the MD-11 and 747-400;
➢ Acoustic nacelles for the MD-11, 757, 767, and 747;
➢ Active turbine cooling for the JT9D engine and the 747;
➢ Composite structures and advanced aluminium alloys for the 757, 767, 747, and the MD-11;
➢ Advanced flightdeck displays for the 757, 767, 747, and 777.

(NASA Office of Aeronautics, FY 1996 Budget Report)

Over US$5 billion was spent at NASA between 1993 and 1998 on aeronautics research, yet no new aircraft program was launched. Seemingly, as Boeing vacillated over where to go with new product decisions its attention became focused again on the subsidy issue. As was argued in Chapter 6, the A380 launch and subsequent sales success caused great dismay to Phil Condit and his colleagues. Hence it is no surprise that in the late 1990s and early 21st century a series of statements from Boeing executives showed renewed concern with the subsidy issue.

The issue really started to boil after the departure of Phil Condit in 2003 and the return from retirement of former McDonnell Douglas CEO, Harry Stonecipher. In interviews with Boeing personnel, the authors have ascertained that Condit had frequently stoked up the subsidy issue, only to then back off when the office of the USTR wanted full backing from Boeing for WTO action. But in September 2004, after series of statements in the media, Boeing pushed Robert Zoelleck, the then-current USTR, to take a case against EU Airbus subsidies to the WTO. The US has alleged that Airbus received at least US$15 billion of launch aid subsidy. The strange thing about the allegation, which itself breaks the 1992 Agreement, is that the transparent Airbus Repayable Launch Investment was clearly in accord with a treaty the US negotiated precisely as a solution to the LCA trade friction. Obviously they now feel that the 1992 Agreement no longer fulfils their requirements.

Airbus, through the offices of the EU, responded with its own WTO case against Boeing subsidies alleging that the American company had received US$23 billion worth of illegal support since 1992. We have discussed some of the forms of US public support for Boeing above. But it should also be mentioned that Boeing's new 787 program is the beneficiary of huge tax breaks. Boeing is seeking US$3.2 billion from the state of Washington in tax breaks, plus US$200m from Kansas. Boeing's partners in Japan are also benefiting from a US$1.4 billion government grant, with the Italian government also chipping in with US$590m. In total this amounts already to more than US$5.5 billion worth of subsidy for the 787. At the very least it seems a strange moment for the US to pursue a WTO course of action when these 787 subsidies, like the Foreign Sales Corporation (FSC) tax breaks, will probably be found to be WTO–illegal.

Conclusion

All of the world's aerospace industries receive financial support from their respective governments in some form or another. In the EU this support is very transparent and consists of repayable grants towards aircraft development costs. Underscoring this is the fact that Airbus has repaid €6 billion to EU governments since 1992. The EU also provides 50% funded research and technology projects through the EC Framework Program. The US federal financial support system is less transparent, with funding coming from a variety of sources via a number of different routes. The traditional form of federal financial support for the civil aircraft industry came from defense procurement. Sometimes aircraft were even produced in government-owned factories but the key benefit came from utilizing technologies, which had been developed for defense products at government expense, on civil aircraft. The US industry also benefited from cash payments paid as overheads on defense contracts and, of course, the huge R&D budget of the Department of Defense. More recently, in the 1990s, the US tried to reinvigorate its industry by pumping billions of dollars into NASA aeronautics research and technology programs. This was done with the express purpose of repulsing the challenge from Airbus. Other US federal financial benefits for the LCA industry come from tax breaks and research projects funded from the Department of Commerce and the FAA.

In the early 1990s the EU and the US resolved the question of financial support through the July 1992 Bilateral Agreement. This reflected the two contrasting ways in which Europe and America supported their industries. The Agreement put limits on the direct supports of the Europeans and the indirect supports of the US industry. Since 1992 the EU has been happy to abide by this agreement and as already stated all Airbus repayable launch investment schemes have been entirely compatible with the 1992 Bilateral.

The last few years have been very difficult for Boeing. Airbus's A380 was successfully launched while both the Boeing 747X and the Sonic Cruiser were withdrawn. In 2003, for the first time ever, Airbus delivered more aircraft than Boeing. Simultaneously, Boeing's defense business was embroiled in a number of scandals, which has undermined the company's reputation in the US. For Boeing Commercial Airplanes the launch of the 787 is a last throw of the dice, in the sense that failure or abandonment of this project would probably destroy the company's credibility in the commercial side of the business. Historically, Boeing has played the subsidy card when it has perceived that it is struggling in terms of business performance. At the present time the subsidy allegations certainly reflect a public relations and political/diplomatic offensive by Boeing. But what remains to be seen is whether the American company has shot itself in the foot. The subsidy allegation may backfire on the company, the 787 project and the Japanese partners. Perhaps what Boeing's search for public funding for the 787 really shows is that the European approach of public/private partnership and repayable government loans is actually quite a good way of promoting the aerospace industry and securing wide economic benefits.

Chapter 8

The Crisis Deepens

Introduction

This chapter assesses some of the self-inflicted wounds that have been evident at Boeing over the last decade. The evidence suggests some endemic weaknesses in the company that will have ongoing consequences. The weaknesses include poor strategy, operational failure, loss of morale and capability and also ethical lapses which have led to criminal charges and convictions against Boeing personnel.

The civil aerospace business carries high risks, despite its oligopolistic structure, and even with a duopoly in the supply side of the large commercial aircraft sector. The risk relates to the huge development cost of new products and the cyclical nature of the air transportation business. With development costs often greater than total company capitalization, one product failure can literally break the bank, as Boeing nearly found to its cost in 1971/1972. The aviation business cycle has a rhythm tuned to the global economy, but can also be impacted by high profile and unpredictable geo-strategic events, like the 9/11 terrorist attacks in 2001. People's willingness to travel by air relates very strongly to their sense of security, which is also affected by health scares, such as the SARS outbreak of 2003. So there is much in the socio-political external environment that can knock a company off track. For the aircraft manufacturer the most worrying scenario is one where it is struggling financially or technologically with a major new program, when recession hits the sector as well. This was the situation which confronted Boeing just as the 747 was entering service in the early 1970s.

Some factors can mitigate the risk of the civil aircraft business and the major players in the sector that are also large defense contractors have often benefited from a counter cyclical defense/civil business process. But on occasion the defense side has turned down at the same time as a civil recession, which happened in the early 1990s.

However, companies also succumb to self-inflicted wounds, as well as the problems that exist externally in the wider business environment. Such injuries can derive from a number of causes, such as: ineffective strategy; poor operational performance; lack of competence and capability; ill-judged decisions; weak or poor morale and corporate culture; basic technological errors; financial irresponsibility, and a host of other defects. As we have seen in previous chapters Douglas, and then McDonnell Douglas, were afflicted by a discrepancy between what sales people offered customers and what engineering and manufacturing could actually deliver. The ill-fated MD-11, which only sold about 200 units, had actually notched up 377 orders by 2001, (Tyson, 1992, p. 191). But the technical deficiencies in the aircraft infuriated launch customer American Airlines, who then reduced its initially large order, which sent a clear message into the market place about the aircraft's capabilities.

The generic and systematic weakness at Boeing Commercial Airplanes has been poor product strategy, especially the failure to invest in new products, coupled with an inability to see the scale of the European challenge and to correctly diagnose the threat posed by Airbus. However, as we shall illustrate below, specific managerial errors in the last decade together with the hire and fire culture of the US company also affected overall corporate performance.

The Business Context

After 1993, the US aerospace industry pursued rapid and far-reaching consolidation and rationalization strategies to overcome the twin problems of global economic recession and post-Cold War defense budget reductions. Between 1990 and 1995, sales of US commercial aircraft fell by some 37%, while military aircraft sales decreased by about 20%. In the 1990s, as Laura Tyson has asserted, the industry confronted a dual challenge. On the one hand it was faced by declining defense budgets, on the other it was posed with the compelling challenge of Airbus Industrie, (Tyson, 1992, p. 155).

Industrial Restructuring

In recent years the global aerospace industry has undergone a complete transformation, with the most prominent example of this the remarkable restructuring process that took place in the US. In America the unification of civil and military aerospace interests, under-pinned by extensive and deep-rooted government research and development programs, was undertaken (at the behest of the US DoD) with remarkable speed in the years between 1992 and 1997. Some 32 defense companies, principally in the aerospace sector, were concentrated into just nine, with the loss of about one million jobs. The unprecedented wave of US aerospace company mergers created two giant corporations, Boeing and Lockheed Martin. As a result of this, the US aerospace prime companies dominated global aerospace markets in terms of sales revenue in the late 1990s.

The New Boeing

In 1996, the announcement of the impending merger of Boeing, an aerospace giant which already dominated the commercial sector, and McDonnell Douglas sharply raised the profile of military aerospace activities within the Boeing organization, and with it the prospect of greatly enhanced opportunities for military/civil synergies and technology transfers. Having already acquired the defense and space business of Rockwell International for US$3.2 billion, the merger with McDonnell Douglas increased the share taken by military aerospace to about 40% of Boeing's US$45 billion revenue for 1997. After the merger was completed Boeing acquired MDC's US$13 billion civil and military business, including US$7 billion worth of military contracts. With sales in 1999 of US$55 billion Boeing emerged as the real colossus of global aerospace and was able to benefit more than ever from defense/commercial synergy and contrasting defense/civil cycles. In 1997 the merger with MDC bequeathed to Boeing the following:

> 84% of all LCA in service (88% including freighters and military variants)
> 60% of current sales of LCA
> 70% of LCA backlog
> Monopoly of both 100 seater and >350 seat transports.

This merger was an example of horizontal integration within the industry, which created a global giant. McDonnell Douglas manufactured the F-15 Eagle and F/A-18E/F Super Hornet fighter aircraft, the C-17 Globemaster III transport, the AH-64 Apache Longbow gunship, and, with British Aerospace, the Harrier II STOVL air support aircraft and T-45 Goshawk trainer. Boeing, while predominantly a civil aerospace manufacturer, had a substantial share of the advanced F-22 Raptor fighter program as well as its own successful AWACS early-warning platforms and H-47 Chinook heavy-lift helicopter. It was also main partner of Sikorsky on the RAH-66 Comanche battlefield helicopter and Bell on the US Marines' V-22 Osprey tilt-rotor military transport. In addition, Boeing was building the X-32, one of two Joint Strike Fighter prototypes battling for a massive 3000-unit contract. To all intents and purposes Boeing looked set to dominate world aerospace but this is not what happened.

A New Number One?

After the US aerospace industry consolidation, many journalists thought the prospects looked bad for Europe. In an article in *The Financial Times* in 1997 Michael Skapinker outlined the competitive threat to European Aerospace posed by the newly merged US industry, with its three giant companies Boeing, Lockheed Martin and Raytheon. Mr Skapinker noted, '… as civil aviation's first century draws to a close it is the US which rules the skies', (*The Financial Times*, 23 September 1997). Regarding the possible threat to Boeing from Airbus's A380, the journalist believed Boeing has a simple answer: 'the stretched 747 would be a relatively cheap way for Boeing, and the US aerospace industry, to maintain their dominance'. But events did not turn out as *The Financial Times* suggested. Two years after the 1997 article was published Lockheed Martin and Raytheon were close to bankruptcy and Airbus was selling more aircraft than Boeing. Some six years later and things are rather different again. Boeing is failing and Airbus is emerging as the dominant player in world civil aerospace. In a 2003 research paper MacPherson and Pritchard comment:

> Today, Boeing is no longer the number one aircraft manufacturer in the world. Airbus holds that prestigious position in every measurable category, including new orders, backlogs and deliveries. Boeing enjoyed more than a 70% market share after the company purchased McDonnell Douglas in the mid 1990s … This share has now fallen below 50%, and the company faces serious problems with aging product lines (i.e. average aircraft design vintages of 28 years, (MacPherson and Pritchard, 2003, p. 3).

This remarkable change has come about because Boeing has made strategic errors and seemingly lost the will to respond to the challenge posed by Airbus. Despite the 787, which is a program being done largely overseas, the strategic drive to invest in new products to ensure future sales seems absent. Again and again senior executives, such as Mike Sears, repeated that what really counted was 'shareholder value'. In an interview in 2001, Sears commented, 'I'm here to tell people we are focused on the job … What's the job? Getting the best returns for our shareholders, (*Sunday Business,* 11 February 2001, p. 23). The 'job' clearly did not include investment in the commercial aircraft part of the business.

At the time of writing (early 2005), much of BCA's product line, the Next-Generation 737, 747-400, and 767, are based on airliners that first flew in the 1960s or 1970s. In the recent hard times that have characterized the aviation industry these older technology aircraft have not sold well. Commentators and customers now question Boeing's commitment to its civil business. Perhaps underscoring this reduced commitment to commercial aircraft Boeing has moved more towards space, as well as defense, in recent years, with civil aircraft revenues dropping below 50% of the company's total in 2002. Nagging doubts persist about whether Boeing wishes to continue to produce civil aircraft in the United States.

Merger Indigestion

The 1997 takeover of McDonnell Douglas created a company of potentially awesome capability. The Boeing senior management were virtually ecstatic. Boeing's Phil Condit and Harry Stonecipher told shareholders:

> *Fortune* magazine called it 'The Sale of the Century'. It is hard for us to contain our enthusiasm regarding the power and potential of the 'new' Boeing, which came into being with the completion of our merger with McDonnell Douglas on August 1, 1997… One could liken the new Boeing to the first freshly painted 747 jumbo jet. We have created the world's largest aerospace company. Now we must prove that this giant new bird will fly farther, faster, higher – and more efficiently – than anything else in the aerospace world. And we will, (1997 Annual Report: Message to Shareholders).

But in retrospect it is clear that the merger generated some significant problems that were not handled well. As is widely recognized, employees in newly merged companies can become unsettled and hostile to their new employer. What begins as cultural differences can easily become cultural incompatibility. The focus on designing and making new organizational forms can also deflect people from the actual business that the company is engaged in. Unless managed carefully the merger process can be highly destructive. Often employees become solely concerned with survival or jockeying for position in the new organization. A former Boeing employee cites the well known 1992 study by Mirvis and Marks which outlined some of the problems that prevent a newly merged enterprise functioning effectively, (Guretsky, 1999, p. 16). She regards the following as relevant to the post-merger Boeing:

Preoccupation	Clash of cultures
Imagining the worst	Us versus them
Stress reactions	Superior versus inferior
Crisis management	Attack and defend
Constricted communication	Win versus lose
Illusion of control	Decisions by coercion, horse trading, and Default, (Mirvis and Marks, 1992, pp. 17-18).

In her study of Boeing, Lt. Col. Joanne Guretsky, also notes the consequences of the post-merger lay offs which she personally observed:

> What puzzled many was the lapse of time between the August 1, 1997, merger, and the sudden announcement of a major re-organization and significant downsizing in the fall of 1998. As can be imagined, the announcement of layoffs, followed by months of waiting to see who would move into what position in the new organizational structure, created significant stress across the company. In some places, work came completely to a halt, and morale sagged as people tried to find positions under managers who didn't even know whether they would have a job in the new corporate structure. Boeing leadership attempted to ease the strain by offering counseling as well as training for new career fields. Some managers from units that were dissolved spent countless hours endeavoring to find "safe places" for their people "until the dust settles, at least". However, with the September announcement that as many as 28,000 positions would be cut by the end of 1999, and even more during the following year, many employees felt a sense of betrayal, (Guretsky, 1999, p. 17).

These comments, from a former employee, highlight the negative effects of the hire and fire culture of the Boeing Company. In the past, on projects such as the 747-400, bringing in tens of thousands of new employees created huge logistical and training problems. Clearly hire and fire was also causing major problems again in the late 1990s. Aerospace is a slow pulse industry, where development and production run over long cycles. The competence of the workforce has to be built up gradually by a process of learning by doing. Shedding large numbers of workers and then bringing a large number back in to ramp up production is risky and likely to cause serious problems.

Managerial Failures and Industrial Meltdown

From the late-1980s Boeing's industrial performance triggered a continuous stream of accusation, speculation, rumour and innuendo concerning poor manufacturing quality, and management and union problems at its main commercial aircraft assembly plants. Accusations, which came from far-and-wide, included complaints from customer airlines, adverse comment and speculation from the aviation industry in general and from a hostile media, and grave accusations from disaffected workers and unions. Far from being revered as an American icon, as in the past, it is now common to see many negative stories in the US media about Boeing.

The most clear cut and costly managerial problems at Boeing in the last decade were evident in a collapse of orderly and efficient production and manufacturing at the Renton and Everett plants in 1997/1998. To be blunt Boeing became incapable of doing the basic bread and butter things that are the bedrock of any successful business. In 2001 *Sunday Business* commented:

> Unfortunately, in the past decade Boeing has produced its fair share of nightmares as well as dreams ... In the late 1990s, in particular, it took big hits from too rapidly ramping up production rates then falling so far out of line with demand that at one stage some of the Seattle assembly lines were stopped altogether to allow the plant to catch its breath, (*Sunday Business*, 11 February 2001, p. 23).

The manufacturing foul-up had major financial consequences. In 1997/1998 Boeing's production crisis robbed the company of the extra profits it should have earned when the market for large commercial aircraft boomed in 1996/1997. On the Next-Generation (NG) 737, which was seeing strong market demand, it was estimated at the time that profitability would not be achieved until 800 units had been produced, (*Flight International,* 2-8 September 1998. p. 67). Bearing in mind that this was a derivative single-aisle aircraft, this was an extraordinary financial failure. A company with a new single-aisle product would hope to break even at 600 units; with a derivative 400 units would be realistic. The production failure and its economic effects also impacted the workforce, as it caused extra lay-offs. Guretsky cites how this issue was presented in the company newspaper, *Boeing News*:

> Even though we're producing commercial airplanes at record levels, and our space and defense businesses remain strong, we lost money last year. So far this year, our financial performance has been disappointing. As a result, our customers are asking us to cut costs

and improve efficiency. Our shareholders are demanding the same. And that's how we'll build a stronger company – one that can provide more opportunities for employees in the future. Unfortunately, reducing costs goes hand-in-hand with reducing employment, (Quoted, Guretsky, 1999, p. 18).

In public statements Boeing suggested that the financial problems resulted from chasing market share and selling aircraft, particularly NG 737s, at rock bottom prices, (*Sunday Business*, 11 February 2001, p. 23). But the truth was that in a single year the company sought to achieve unprecedented increases in production, while also completing development of four new derivative models, which it failed to do. But in the attempt to achieve these objectives production chaos was created with operating costs going sky high. By the time the problem was being resolved the Asian financial crisis had hit demand and the company had too much capacity again, (*Sunday Business* 21 June 1998, p. 4*). Flight International* identified the real cause of the financial haemorrhage:

What went wrong and what action is being taken to make sure it never happens again? These are the questions being asked by Boeing and the investment community as the company begins recovering from a dire production crisis that continues to wreak havoc with its financial performance, (*Flight International*, 2-8 September 1998. p. 67).

The problems of 1997/1998 were not really about the workforce or its capability. Boeing suffered an extraordinary failure of logistical capability caused by bad management, where inability to track inventory and incompatible computer systems put the whole production system in jeopardy.

Manufacturing problems at Boeing's production facilities in the US came to a head in 1998. Reports in the aviation press (See, for example, *Flug Review,* August 1998, p. 4) painted a picture of a company in turmoil in respect of production and manufacture. Delays at assembly plants which had cost the company dearly in 1997 (reportedly US$2.6 billion in late delivery penalties) continued into 1998. It was reported that the wrong wings were assembled to one 737 and that major assemblies were damaged in transit from Boeing's plant in Wichita to Renton. Another aircraft received the wrong paint finish. Half finished airliners, awaiting supplier parts were reportedly being left unprotected and unpainted at sites in the Puget Sound area. The then President and Chief Executive of Boeing Commercial Airplanes, Ron Woodard, initially tried to reject the manufacturing incidents as being nothing unusual in the context of several billion parts being moved around and assembled into hundreds of complete aircraft each year. However, the financial institutions and many individual shareholders did not take the same view. Indeed, in the spring of 1998 investors were calling for the head of CEO Condit, as Boeing credibility and stock continued to nosedive.

In procurement, as the company sought to ramp up production, Boeing discovered that suppliers it had previously relied upon, had moved out of aerospace or had other customer priorities. In effect Boeing had lost control of its supply chain, with a chronic shortage of parts for the 747-400 line. In a quite unprecedented move, head of commercial airplanes, Ron Woodard, actually stopped 747 production after he had admitted to journalists that it was, 'out of control'. But having shut down the 747 line it became clear that NG 737 production was in chaos as well. Ultimately, Woodard paid for the crisis with his job, but in fact the faults went higher up in the company.

The Production Crisis and Lean Manufacturing

In the mid-1990s Boeing were introducing a new form of production and manufacturing control to ensure that the configuration of aircraft offered to customers could actually be built in the company's factories at a sensible cost. Boeing had learned a hard lesson in this respect on the 747-400. In essence, options and customizations on aircraft were being offered to customers with no thought to the logistical or cost aspects of production. There was no tailoring of specific 'business streams' to different categories of order. The system was ad hoc, chaotic and highly expensive. On the 747-400, in a logistics and cost-control nightmare, the first three aircraft produced each had engines from a different manufacturer, (*Flight International,* 26 August - 2 September 1998, p. 29).

The systems that Boeing was trying to replace had evolved haphazardly since 1945. By the 1990s 1500 legacy computer systems existed in Boeing plants with single programs having as many as 15 separate bills of material. In order to rectify this, Boeing managers introduced Define and Control Aircraft Configuration (DCAC) and Manufacturing Resource Management (MRM). Using powerful new hardware and software to track inventory and store configuration data, business streams were linked to a single source of product data, with library information concerning modifications and service bulletin data, (*Flight International,* 26 August - 2 September 1998, p. 29). As a result, part of the define and build process was automated as pre-existing configurations were matched to systematized customer requirements. In short a more disciplined approach to configuration was linked to greater knowledge and control of inventory and capabilities.

However, new systems such as DCAC and MRM require cultural change in the workforce and a good deal of training. In the early phase of such a change, process production may actually slow as learning difficulties are overcome. But, as we have seen, in 1996/1997 Boeing tried to massively accelerate production while in the middle of implementing the new system. The result was an industrial meltdown, with out-of-sequence production and huge increases in manufacturing costs. Some estimates suggested that production costs had increased by a massive 500%. The damage to Boeing's reputation was huge: 'By the time order was restored, the company had lost most of its credibility on Wall Street', (*Business Week Online*, 15 December 2003).

Consequences of the Production Failure

As well as damaging Boeing's esteem and reputation, the production crisis also led to a charge of US$1.6 billion in the fourth quarter of 1997. What should have been a period of profitability turned to one of loss. Next-Generation 737s, which were selling well, were being produced at a loss. Top aerospace analyst Wolfgang Demisch referred to the situation as one of 'profitless prosperity', (*Washington Post*, 18 January 1998). Arguably this was the decisive catalyst in the ensuing downturn in Boeing's fortunes. After the absorption of MDC many in Europe were fearful of the corporate power of the new US$55 billion company. But the giant failed to achieve. By any standards, the stewardship of recently departed CEO Phil Condit must be judged a failure. In 1998 Ron Woodard was fired and the company announced the layoff of 48,000 workers, as shares crashed 17% in one day. Chief Financial Officer Debbie Hopkins soon followed Woodard. In addition to the production debacle the company was perceived to be late in responding to the Asian crisis and instead of an orderly reduction in output the reaction looked like panic.

Manufacturing problems again came to a head in February 2000 when workers in Seattle took strike action. The 45-day strike was based on complaints from workers that they were suffering health problems and stress from working too much overtime and to a production schedule set by Boeing management that was beyond the capacity of the assembly lines.

In an interview in 1998, former Boeing Commercial Airplanes head, Ron Woodard, acknowledged that going to the market earlier with the Next-Generation 737 would have lessened the problems caused by the production ramp up of 1997, (*Flight International,* 2-8 September 1998, p. 67). The reason Boeing delayed was that profit margins on the 30-year-old 737 Classic were very high. In essence, short-term shareholders interests were regarded as more important than longer-term strategic objectives. But the chaos of 1997/1998 cost the company dear.

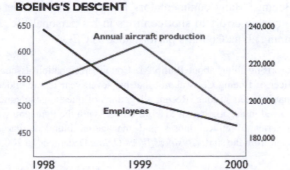

Figure 8.1   The Impact of the Asian Crisis on Boeing in 1998
Credit: BBC online.

Strategic Failure

After the problems of 1997/1998 Boeing seemed to lose its way and it came second to Airbus in sales for 1998, 1999, 2001, 2002 and 2003. In the meantime the 747X and the Sonic Cruiser were abandoned and the JSF contest was lost. Strategically, Boeing's last few years have been a disaster. In an extraordinary lack of foresight, CEO Phil Condit apparently believed that Airbus would never launch the A380 program, (*Business Week Online,* 15 December 2003). The same *Business Week Online* article charts Boeing's descent:

> While Airbus got bigger, Boeing stagnated. The failure to formulate a strategy that could keep up with an emboldened Airbus began to tell as Boeing fell behind in both technology and manufacturing efficiency during the '90s. Boeing, once the manufacturing marvel of the world, now spent 10% to 20% more than Airbus to build a plane. The loss in market share – from nearly 70% in 1996 to roughly 50% today – has marked an astonishing reversal, (*Business Week Online,* 15 December 2003).

Looking for profits outside commercial aircraft Condit supported the purchase of Hughes Space & Communications for US$3.75 billion and Jeppersen-Sanderson Inc for US$1.5 billion in 2000. The former CEO thought that space was a sure bet. But in 2003 he informed employees at the Boeing Everett plant that the space market, 'did not turn out to be what we thought it was going to be, and we didn't perform', (*Business Week Online*, 15 December 2003). In 2003 Boeing took a US$1.1 billion charge against the failing space market. Perhaps related to inadequate due diligence, the Hughes-designed satellites that Boeing had been trying to sell showed serious quality shortcomings. The space venture has not gone well.

Condit's Departure

In December 2003, after seven years in the job, Phil Condit resigned as CEO and Chairman of Boeing. Many commentators in the business media catalogued his failings, from strategic errors to shortcomings in his personal life. *Business Week Online* was scathing about Condit's performance as CEO:

> The really surprising thing about Philip M. Condit's resignation as chairman and chief executive officer of Boeing Co. was not that his seven-year tenure ended so abruptly on Dec. 1, but that it lasted so long. Recent allegations of questionable conduct by a Boeing executive involved in negotiating an $18 billion deal with the Pentagon was only the latest mishap in a series of ethical lapses and managerial blunders that marred Condit's tumultuous reign from the start, *(Business Week Online* December 15 2003).

According to the same magazine Condit was simply not cut out for the job:

The story of Philip Murray Condit, 62, is the tale of a manager promoted beyond his competence and blind to his own shortcomings. The skills that made him a brilliant engineer – obsessive problem solving and an ability to envision elegant design solutions – were of less use in an executive position. Although always a bold visionary, Condit was frequently indecisive and isolated as a CEO – in stark contrast to his predecessors, (*(Business Week Online*, 15 December 2003).

It is obviously unfair and incorrect to blame one individual for Boeing woes, but Condit's stewardship of Boeing was failure-ridden and crisis-laden. Within a year of his appointment the production meltdown occurred and soon afterwards Boeing lost the number one spot in commercial aircraft to Airbus. It is staggering to realize that just seven years ago in 1997 Boeing's revenues from commercial aircraft sales were about six times those of Airbus, at US$26.9 billion compared to US$4.6 billion, (*Flight International,* 2-8 September 1998, p. 50). By 2003 they were close to parity.

One of Condit's strategic objectives was to make Boeing less dependent on commercial aircraft sales by growing the space and defense business. But, as in the past, defense work was sought which supported the commercial arm. This was very clear with the contentious USAF tanker leasing deal, which would have given Boeing US$22 billion in cash and ensured the survival of the failing 767 line, as 100 of the aircraft would have been required as air-to-air refuelling tankers. But under Phil Condit, Boeing even managed to alienate the US DoD by being caught engaging in unethical and illegal business practices. Strategic failure was compounded by scandal and corruption.

The Whiff of Scandal

In a book that was to have been published in November 2003, Mike Sears of Boeing and his co-author, Thomas Schweich state, 'either you are ethical or you are not. You have to make the decision; all of us do. And there is no in-between', (*The Economist,* 29 November 2003). Shortly after review copies were circulated, Mike Sears was fired for misconduct and the book was withdrawn.

After the Enron scandal, corporate governance issues have been very much to the fore in the US. Mike Sears was fired because he allegedly discussed future employment at Boeing with a Pentagon official, who was then working on the USAF procurement of 100 leased Boeing KC-767 tankers. The Pentagon official (Darleen Druyun) subsequently went to work for Boeing's missile division on a US$250,000 a year contract. But since then Ms. Druyun has been jailed for nine months for admitting a criminal conflict of interest in her work on the tanker lease deal. Ms. Druyun, in her role as chief of Air Force procurement, was pushing contracts towards Boeing in return for the offer of a job and jobs for other members of her family. She also increased the value of the tanker contract as a sweetener for her new employer. Mike Sears, the Boeing executive who negotiated with Mrs. Druyun, also pleaded guilty to a related offence. At the time the scandal broke in the news media Mr. Sears insisted that he had done nothing wrong but in February 2005 he was sentenced to four months prison and fined US$250,000 by a US court, (*Wall Street Journal*, 21 February 2005).

In July 2003, the US Air Force announced that it was barring Boeing from future rocket work and revoking US$1 billion-worth of contracts. The work was reassigned to Lockheed Martin after it had emerged that Boeing had resorted to industrial espionage to win the contracts during a procurement competition held in 1998. Lockheed Martin had successfully sued Boeing for acquiring some 25,000 confidential documents during the competition phase. The stolen information was thought to have helped Boeing to better position itself for 21 out of 28 military satellite launches in the Air Force's Expendable Launch Vehicle program. Boeing was forced to apologize publicly for the affair after the US Air Force had announced that Boeing had committed serious and substantial violations of federal law. All this came immediately on top of other incidents of unethical business conduct. Only seven months earlier, the general Accounting Officer found that Boeing had obtained and misused proprietary information from Raytheon as the two companies competed for a missile defense contract. The US Justice Department launched a criminal investigation into the Lockheed Martin matter. Subsequently Boeing employees were indicted by a grand jury for theft of trade secrets, (*The Economist*, 29 January 2003). Because of these shortcomings Boeing hired former Senator Warren Rudman in 2003 to look into ethical issues at the company.

As well as the existing cases it appears that Lockheed Martin may seek to bring charges of criminal racketeering against Boeing. Lawyers for Lockheed Martin have outlined this possibility in court papers filed in Florida. The company is claiming that the offences uncovered in its suit against Boeing over the stealing of business secrets and the subsequent cover up represent a violation of the US Racketeer Influenced and Corrupt Organizations Act. Lockheed Martin is seeking further evidence of criminal acts stemming from the continuing US investigations into the Boeing KC-767 tanker lease deal. Court documents filed in Florida also mention a separate federal grand jury investigation in Los Angeles involving Boeing. As *The Seattle Weekly* comments: 'Lockheed [Martin] maintains that incidents related to these cases can be linked to show a 14-year "pattern" of illegal activity by Boeing', (*Seattle Weekly*, 1-7 December 2004).

A Deeper Malaise

Subsequent revelations suggest that the scandal ran deeper than contact between Boeing's Chief Financial officer and just one DoD official. In November 2004 Air Force Secretary James Roche and Marvin Sambur, the chief of Air Force Procurement, announced their resignations over the tanker scandal. Publicly, Roche was making statements about the need for more competition in US defense procurement. But in private Roche was lobbying for Boeing on the tanker deal and rubbishing the European competitor EADS, (*The Financial Times*, 24 November 2004). As a result US Senator John McCain is demanding a wider investigation into the scandal and the right to impose financial penalties against Boeing. But the really bad news for Boeing is that the scandal compelled the US to pull the plug on the tanker deal. The bail out of the 767 has been terminated. There will now be a new competition with Boeing's rival EADS seeking to make a case for the Airbus A330 tanker. After what commenced on the previous competition it will now be imperative that the US DoD gives the EADS bid a fair and scrupulous evaluation.

The US Defense/Industrial Base

After the major consolidation of the 1990s in the US defense industrial base, many commentators now argue that defense industrial power is too concentrated in America. Effectively there is only competition between two or three industrial giants for major programs, while a small number of supplier companies compete for lesser work packages. This is good news for the incumbent firms, but bad news for the US government and taxpayer. The only way out of this conundrum is to open up the US market to external competition.

The need to open up the US defense market is graphically illustrated by the Boeing tanker scandal. Emails revealed by Senator John McCain illustrate a cosy and close relationship between DoD officials and Boeing, with the DoD procurement officials lobbying hard for the Chicago-based company and pouring scorn on competitors such as EADS, (*The Financial Times,* 24 November, 2004). What Boeing has done with its behaviour in the tanker scandal is show why it must now be subject to genuine competition. It has actually begun to undermine its protected position in the US defense market and in the process created widespread popular and journalistic hostility. To underscore the point, in 2003 *Forbes* magazine ranked Phil Condit one of the worst and most overpaid bosses in the US corporate arena, (*The Seattle Weekly*, 3-9 December 2003).

Conclusion

Boeing was once a great company, led by engineers and managers who espoused a tough but fair code of ethics. Statements of the company founder Bill Boeing show the direction he wanted to see:

> I've tried to make the men around me feel as I do, that we are embarked as pioneers upon a new science and industry in which our problems are so new and unusual that it behooves no one to dismiss any novel idea with the statement that 'It can't be done.' Our job is to keep everlastingly at research and experiment, to adopt our laboratory results and those of other laboratories to production as soon as practicable, to let no improvement in flying and flying equipment pass us by, (Quoted, Guretsky, 1999, p. 15).

In the early decades the search for innovation and the desire to be best was apparent. But also through clever strategic judgement after 1945 Boeing positioned itself skilfully in the new world of civil jet manufacture so that it could further develop technologies used on military programs. But the company also exhibited daring and élan. The transition from the Dash 80 to the 707 was far from smooth, with the need for rapid and radical redesigns ongoing. Also, Boeing had a wily and skilful competitor in Douglas.

After the 707 Boeing was faster than Douglas in developing new models and therefore became the first company to benefit from the family concept, as it reaped the rewards from the 727, 737 and 747. The European challenge failed not only because the UK's pioneering Comet had a fatal flaw but also because there were too many small and competing European programs that could never be profitable. But then, just as the new threat to Boeing from Airbus emerged, innovation stopped. The 757 and 767 were not radical steps forward and the threat from the Airbus A300 was underestimated. Similarly, the challenge from the Airbus single-aisle family was ducked. Innovation and new engineering was evident on the 777 but one type does not make a product line. In essence the product strategy became paralysed as extracting cash from existing aircraft types was seen as more important than investment for the future.

Overall, Boeing has exhibited a lack of strategic vision that has pushed the company backwards in the competition with Airbus and also resulted in major setbacks within the US. The lack of investment in new product is the key factor and it has allowed Airbus to dominate the technical agenda. From the point of view of the American national interest Boeing is declining in importance as it has failed to renew its technical capabilities and is also exporting US jobs to Asia. The industrial crisis of 1997/1998 further suggests critical failures of management. But the recent scandals suggest that something even more profound may be wrong. Boeing has the air of a company in crisis; a company that has lost its way. Engaging in behaviour that has alienated the US DoD is a major strategic error.

Boeing failing's are bad news for the US government, taxpayers, air passengers and airlines. Under Phil Condit's leadership everything seemed to go awry. The

1990s saw an accelerated decline in commercial market share as the past failure to invest in new product begun to impact in the market. But in the early 21st century major strategic blunders have fundamentally weakened the company. The forthcoming 787 may see Boeing moving back to health in commercial airplanes but by itself it is not enough.

At the present time the financial returns of the Boeing company would seem to cast doubt on the thesis advanced here. But we contend that Boeing's failures will exact a heavy commercial impact in the future. With more dependence on defense work and a weakened position in the civil market Boeing will be vulnerable to future defense cuts and to more open competition in the US military market. The scale of borrowing and debt that is financing the current defense build up in the US is unsustainable. But the most extraordinary error is the transfer of capability to rivals. What remains an utter mystery is why Boeing should seek to place so much of the 787 work overseas and in the process equip Japan to be a major challenger in aeronautics in the 21st century. For Airbus it may mean that the next significant new challenge exists in North East Asia and not the United States. Ironically, if Boeing continues to export jobs to Asia it may be that Airbus will increase its investment in America to access the US skills and competencies that Boeing no longer appears to need.

Chapter 9

Postscript: A Boeing Comeback?

Introduction

This book has advanced the thesis that the Boeing Company has lost strategic leadership in the commercial aircraft industry to Airbus. The argument and analysis cover a 30-year period during which time a new entrant firm gradually came to parity and then dominance over the leading incumbent company. To emphasize the point, Airbus had a 53% market share in 2004. The explanation given for this transformation is that Boeing pursued a conservative and self-defeating product development strategy, eschewing investment in new models for cash gains to shareholders and controversial share buy-back schemes.

In the early part of 2005 the crisis and strategic failures at Boeing identified in the last chapter appeared to be continuing. In February, Boeing rolled out its latest derivative aircraft, the 777-200LR. This ultra long-range derivative of the 777 is another development of a product originally conceived in 1988 as the 767X. This fifth instalment of the 777 is not a brand new aircraft and at the time of the roll out had secured just five firm sales, (*Flight International*, 22-28 February 2005). However, the public relations that attached to the 777-200LR roll out were brilliant. The world's media were convinced that the 777-200LR was a completely new aircraft. Thus, even if not in the domain of real products, Boeing had at least begun to fight back in the realm of media relations. But the real test is yet to come; which is delivering on the promises made on the 787.

Reprise

In March 2005 it was announced that Boeing's CEO Harry Stonecipher was being forced to resign because of an affair he had been conducting with a Boeing lobbyist, Debra Peabody. This was yet another mishap for the company that had actually brought Stonecipher back to repair the damage done in the later years of Phil Condit's reign. Because of scandals two CEOs had been forced to go in just 15 months. Ironically, Mr Stonecipher fell foul of the strict new ethical code he had introduced into the company. One can see laudable consistency in the decision to terminate the CEO, but sadly it also appeared to be another major disaster for the company. However, it must be acknowledged that despite this setback Boeing has since exhibited signs of recovery. This final chapter assesses the company's prospects in the light of recent events. We investigate here whether Boeing's apparent recovery is real and sustainable. We further seek to assess the long-term outlook in the Airbus/Boeing competition.

Recovery?

The perception that Boeing is undergoing a recovery took hold in the second quarter of 2005. The clearest sign of a recovery was in sales of its new 787 aircraft. At the end of the first quarter of 2005, sales of the 787 were just 64, (www.speednews.com/lists/1Q05O&D.pdf). But by mid-June gross sales had risen to over 250 units. Boeing clearly had a blistering second quarter.

The Power of Public Relations

Economists sometimes distinguish between intrinsic and extrinsic competitiveness. Intrinsic competitiveness is embedded in a company's core skills and competencies; it refers to technological and managerial capabilities. Extrinsic competitiveness concerns the reputation of the company and the role of marketing and communications in securing the strength of the brand and image, (Bowonder and Rao, 1993, pp. 5-47). There is no doubt that Boeing has always been highly skilled in the extrinsic dimension, although the scandals on the defense side of the business overdrew even that capability in 2003.

In the process of renewal in Boeing's reputation that has taken place in the second quarter of 2005 it is very clear that an excellent communications strategy has been executed. Boeing has been very active in the media, amplifying and pushing its own achievements very hard. Also Boeing spokesmen have constantly been on hand to downplay or neutralize any major positive publicity for Airbus. This is an entirely legitimate form of business practice. However, it can also be misleading. The real performance indicators hidden behind a publicity blitz can be very different from the public perception. Therefore we pose the question: how real is the Boeing revival?

The Role of Leadership

One real change in Boeing in 2005 concerns the role of leadership. In the last chapter we analyzed some of the strategic errors of former CEO Phil Condit. With every passing week it becomes clearer how significant those errors were. Both on the WTO question and also on the issue of new product development. Mr Condit appears to have been indecisive and prone to prevarication. His replacement, Harry Stonecipher, obviously put some real bite and determination into strategic policy direction. Although, paradoxically it was Mr Stonecipher who presided over McDonnell Douglas's decline in the civil market leading to its demise in 1997. In March 2005 the new CEO departed because of a scandal, but Boeing have continued to exhibit a new focus and sense of purpose in the wake of Stonecipher's departure.

One area where renewed vigour has been evident has been in sales and marketing. In 2004 Boeing replaced its existing head of sales with Scott Carson, the head of the Boeing Internet Connexion business. With reference to the Airbus/Boeing sales competition Carson boldly proclaimed that 'We will beat them this year', (*Business Week,* 13 April, 2005). As of mid-year the situation did look favourable to the US company, but Boeing did not do as well with orders booked at the Paris Air Show as many pundits predicted. At Le Bourget, Airbus secured 279 orders and commitments, vs. 148 for Boeing. Moreover, a high profile Boeing sale to Air Canada has now been lost due to threats of industrial action by Air Canada flight crew.

Nevertheless, Boeing had a very good half-year, particularly with sales of the new 787. Boeing's sales victory with Air Canada unsettled Airbus, as did the sale of 787s to long-term Airbus customer, Northwest. Interestingly, strong rumours about heavy discounting by Boeing appeared at the time of the Northwest deal. In the past a constant Boeing jibe against Airbus has been that the European company offered planes at loss-making prices. Yet it now seems that Boeing is the one going to the wire on price. Market share now seems the major strategic objective. As one Boeing executive commented, 'We were going pretty deep there…We knew this would be a huge win', (*Business Week,* 13 April 2005).

As fate would have it, Airbus's charismatic commercial chief, John Leahy, was indisposed due to illness during the key later stages of these critical campaigns. It is well known that the Airbus sales chief is always closely involved at the key points in sales campaigns and he has an enviable reputation for winning the day. Certainly his absence will have weakened Airbus and helped the Boeing cause.

Altogether the Boeing sales success of 2005 has definitely begun to refocus the perception of the media. The previously critical *Business Week* commented, 'But since the first of the year, Boeing commercial airplane division has been regaining its mojo. The Northwest Airlines sale offers the perhaps the most telling example of a company intensely focused on reclaiming leadership of the commercial jet industry', (*Business Week,* 13 April, 2005).

787: Flattering to Deceive?

The perception of a Boeing revival is very much tied to the new 787 project. The 787 has benefited from an excellent marketing campaign. A number of the aircraft's features have caught the media's and the public's imagination. The 787 offers reduced cabin altitude pressure at cruise (6000 ft) and also increased cabin humidity. Both features are presented as providing enhanced comfort for passengers. In addition, Boeing has made many claims about the improved economic performance of the new plane, based mainly on the reduced weight of the aircraft structure, secured by replacing aluminium with composite materials.

The company is talking of a 20% reduction in fuel costs. For the customer this all sounds highly attractive. But is it that simple? As the experience of McDonnell Douglas with the MD-11 illustrates, the aircraft business has frequently seen engineering teams fail to deliver the performance levels that sales and marketing have promised to customers. In addition there is some sleight of hand here, as the real improvement in performance offered by the 787 may have more to do with the new engines than the composite structure. In fact General Electric (Rolls-Royce is the other engine choice) is offering 15% less fuel burn than on previous wide-body engines, (http://en.wikipedia.org/wiki/General_Electric_GENX).

Issues with Composites

The 50% composite content and in particular the composite fuselage of the 787 presents enormous challenges to Boeing engineers and manufacturing teams. As 787 Vice President Michael Bair posed the question, 'Can we build the 787 at production volumes?' (Quoted, *Business Week,* 20 June, 2005). In fact Boeing engineers did not want to go down the composite route. Manufacturing large pieces of composite structure is difficult, as the process is complex and dependent on high skill levels amongst employees. In order to produce the huge fuselage barrels, composite tape, woven from ultra-strong polymer fibres, is soaked in liquefied polymers and then baked in an autoclave. The process requires a craft-like skill level and is hard to automate. Ensuring consistent quality is difficult as Boeing has already found on the first few fuselage barrels it fabricated. The disadvantages of composite for mass production are described by Vern Raburn, the CEO of Eclipse Aviation:

> Perhaps the largest disadvantage to composites is their total unsuitability to high-volume production rates. All current aviation composite systems are what are called "thermoset" systems. That means that the material must be "cured" at high temperatures and pressures. For high-volume/low-cost work, the auto industry uses a "thermoplastic" system that cures rapidly in molds. This process is basically like injection molding of plastics. The FAA has never certified such a system for aviation usage. Furthermore, we believe the cost of developing and certifying a thermoset system would require a major investment as well as add significant risk to the certification process. So while composites have both an appropriate application in some areas of aviation (low-volume production and/or non-structural parts) and a very bright future in aviation, we believe strongly that aluminum is the best choice for a high-volume jet such as the Eclipse 500, (Quoted, *Aluminum Now,* September/October 2002.

Damage Detection

Boeing is claiming that the 787 will need less maintenance checks than a metallic aircraft. It has been suggested that the first major structural examination of the aircraft might not be necessary for 12 years, because of less concern over corrosion, (*Business Week,* 20 June 2005). But this view neglects a key fact about composites. Damage to metallic structures is easy to see, although assessing the effects of the damage is often complex. Much is known about fracture mechanics and the impact of loads and stress on cracks in metals. Less is known about composite. But the bigger problem is that damage to composite materials is more difficult to detect and interpret. Impact damage may not be visible and moreover, the real structural harm to composite material after an impact may be physically removed from the actual impact point.

With a composite fuselage there are certain to be bumps and shunts on the ground and ramp from service vehicles causing varying degrees of damage to the structure. Because of this, operators of the 787 will need to implement a vigilant regime of damage inspection and investigation. The evaluation of complex composite structures often requires labour-intensive, expensive methods because of multiple failure modes, difficulty detecting damage, and the large scale of the structures. To get around this the only course of action is investment in expensive ultra sound and laser doppler test equipment. But even worse when composite structure is damaged it is costly to repair.

The Environment

In many respects graphite or carbon fibre composite is an environmental disaster. Consider the following example. Some years ago Raytheon/Beech produced a composite business turbo-prop called the Starship. The plane was a commercial failure and Raytheon/Beech bought most of the 50 aircraft back from customers. To the dismay of environmentalists these aircraft were burned. Carbon fibre composite cannot be recycled and also requires high energy levels in production. Altogether the following environmental and cost disadvantages of the material are evident:

> ➢ High materials cost leading to high production costs;
> ➢ Anisotropic behaviour causing complex design and increased production costs;
> ➢ New bonding and repair technologies with increased maintenance costs;
> ➢ Complex failure modes and damage development increasing maintenance costs;
> ➢ Virtually impossible to recycle causing high disposal and end of life cost.

In an age where environmental issues are so prominent Boeing will surely face taxing questions on the issue of the non-recyclability of its new high-volume composite aircraft.

Galvanic Corrosion

Joining materials together that have different electro-chemical characteristics is problematic because it causes galvanic corrosion. Galvanic corrosion occurs when materials of different corrosive weakness (an anode and a cathode) are in close proximity in conjunction with an electrolyte, i.e. water. The flow of ions from one material to the other causes the corrosion. Materials engineers rely on a chart called the Galvanic Series to see which materials are bound to generate a corrosive reaction. Graphite composite is highly cathodic and not prone to corrosion, aluminium is highly anodic. Composite graphite and aluminium in close proximity with water is a classic mix for corrosion; acting essentially as a battery.

On the 787 the high levels of graphite composite in the structure, coupled with the promised high level of cabin humidity has created a major problem regarding the use of aluminium. Despite the possibility of placing sealant between the aluminium and the composite, Boeing has felt it necessary to replace large amounts of aluminium with titanium, which is much less corrosion prone. Some comments by Boeing engineers suggest that as much as 20% of the 787 structure may have to be of titanium. Titanium is fractionally heavier, but much more expensive than aluminium. Manufacturing costs are particularly high. Therefore meeting the originally targeted costs for the 787 will be near impossible.

Behind Schedule?

At the 2005 Paris Air Show, Richard Aboulafia, Vice President, Analysis at Teal Group, predicted that the new Boeing 787 would be about 12 months behind schedule, (www.leeham.net/filelib/ScottsColumn62805.pdf). The Le Bourget Teal announcement was flatly denied by Boeing, but interestingly Teal is usually very supportive to the US company, so its announcement had credibility. There is no way of validating Mr Aboulafia's prediction, but it squares with what is being said around the engineering rumour mill on the composites issue and also with opinions being expressed in www discussion groups. In the second quarter of 2005 Boeing have very much been in the honeymoon period of the 787 project, where all kinds of good news is being announced prior to the program hitting the inevitable snags that arise as engineering and manufacturing teams move towards actual fabrication and integration.

The globally-distributed system of production on the 787, similar to the Airbus system that Boeing previously ridiculed, will present serious logistical and organizational challenges before it beds down. Few things in life are certain, but one sure bet is that major aircraft engineering programs fall behind schedule and go over budget. Complexity adds to the problems. As more aircraft and systems' content are outsourced, the primes such as Boeing become hostage to the performance of strategic partners and suppliers. With 65% of the 787 outsourced, Boeing is especially vulnerable in this respect. All of these factors make us believe that Richard Aboulafia's predictions are correct.

Another problem for Boeing with 65% of the 787 outsourced is that its own engineers are worried about the future of the company. As the *Chicago Tribune* noted, '[Boeing] Engineers working on the 787 program fear that the mass outsourcing of design work is causing a brain drain … Inside and outside Boeing, concern is rising that the company could lose its capacity to build an airplane. It might also create a new competitor that one day could take away its market share, as Airbus did…', (*Chicago Tribune*, 23 February, 2005).

Battle Joined

For the last four years Airbus has sold more aircraft than Boeing, climbing to a 53% share of the market in 2004. In 2005 it is harder to call, but Boeing may well win the sales battle. But what of the future? We see the bandwidth in market share between the two companies as quite narrow, probably in the range 45%–55% share. We do not envisage hegemonic market dominance in the range of 60%–70% share for either company. For Boeing much depends on delivering the promised performance for the 787. But the real snags with the program are only just emerging and manufacturing costs will be high.

Of course, as we saw in Chapter 7, the US$ 3.2bn tax breaks from the state of Washington and the US$1.5bn from the Japanese government for the 787 will give the program a major financial advantage. Although, this begs the question of why the US has taken WTO action against the EU over Airbus subsidies? According to Aboulafia, the WTO action is essentially a delaying tactic to slow down the introduction of the new Airbus A350. Again, such assertions are impossible to verify, but it is interesting that the US side has linked its willingness to negotiate to the question of EU launch investment for the A350. The belligerent US tone on government support for the 350 has had an effect in Europe. But so far the EU is standing firm.

A380 and the 787

A number of commentators have spuriously evaluated the prospects of the 787 and A380 as a question of the hub versus spoke concept of aviation growth. This is wrong because it is abundantly clear that the future will be characterized by both. These aircraft are not competitors; they are designed for different markets. A380 is a response to some key facts about global society. Many of the world's air passengers live in the great urban conurbations, like Hong Kong, Beijing, London, Los Angeles or Sydney. These individuals will continue to travel hub-to-hub. In the developing world, where the greatest air travel growth is expected, cities will continue to increase in size. Urbanization and economic development go hand in hand. The number of big hubs will increase. Expansion in this traffic cannot be accommodated by simply increasing the number of flights and aircraft in the system. The number of high-density routes where there are slot restrictions will continue to grow. Of course there are passengers looking for convenient smaller city-to-city spokes, but the world aviation system cannot keep remorselessly adding city pairs. Environmental and economic factors will preclude it.

With respect to the A380 the future prospects of the aircraft are chiefly in Airbus's hands. If A380 delivers its promised performance and high in-service reliability it will be great success with sales in the region of 750 to 900 over the next 20 years. Some critics believe that the market and the system is not ready for A380, but it is more prepared than it was for the Boeing 747 35 years ago. As with the 747, A380 can make its own market it if delivers what the customer wants.

In June 2004, Richard Aboulafia, Aaron Gellman and other colleagues released a Shadow Report on the A380, (www.leeham.net/default.asp?Page=27). The Boeing-funded report, actually written in 2002, was released in 2004 in order to do maximum damage to A380's prospects and to back up the US move to a WTO case. The report underscores Boeing's point-to-point fragmentation philosophy and assumes a market of only 496 for the Airbus plane over a 20-year period. Intriguingly, Mr Aboulafia, co-author of the report which says that A380 will make a loss of US$9bn, predicted in his Le Bourget statement that A380 will 'transition from a revenue drain to a revenue contributor' during the life of the program, (Hamilton, 2005, p. 2). As Scott Hamilton points out, this is 'puzzling'. In fact the so-called Shadow Report has a number of bizarre aspects. Inter alia it:

> Understates historic load factors;
> Uncritically accepts the fragmentation philosophy;
> Fails to understand the learning curve effect on manufacturing costs which can go down dramatically as unit number increase;
> Assumes a retirement age of 25 years on 747s, when Asian and Middle Eastern airlines often retire them between 10–15 years.

The truth, of course, is that predictions on aircraft sales and financial success are speculative and tenuous. In the early 1970s the prospects for the 747 looked extremely bleak. It would have been a bold analyst to predict sales of 1,500 units. To return to A380 we contend that the future of the aircraft lies in Airbus's hands. Contrary to earlier press statements Boeing has not abandoned plans for a new derivative of the 747-400. Airlines with high-density routes and restricted slots, such as British Airways and JAL, may compel Boeing to offer a rival to A380. But we contend that if the Airbus icon delivers all that has been promised these customers will feel compelled to buy it.

Finale

On the 787 Boeing has created an aura of radical technology around the aircraft concept, but this is largely mythical. In earlier computer-generated images of the plane both the tail section and the nose had a futuristic appearance. But as the design became frozen and the aerodynamical constrictions became clear these radical features have gone. The idea that the 50% use of composites is radical is misleading, as composites has been around in the aircraft business for a long time. It is the 'spin' that has been at the cutting edge. However, being radical in the sphere of public relations alone will soon not be enough. Over the last 35 years Airbus's dogged persistence in building and selling commercial jet aircraft has brought it to parity and then leadership over its great American rival. For the US company to regain its crown it will require more than good public relations. What is needed is sustained investment in a new family of advanced technology aircraft. Hearing in June 2005 that Boeing has just announced another 10 million US$2.7bn share buy back scheme does not square with the requirement for major product investment. As the aerospace analyst Scott Hamilton notes, the money Boeing has spent buying back its own stock – more than US$9 billion since December 2000 – 'could easily have funded an entirely new airplane,' (*The Daily Herald*, 29 June 2005). The 787 is an interesting riposte to Airbus, but other behaviours at Boeing, particularly the share buyback and the 65% outsourcing of the 787 seem to us to be strategic blunders. However, only the future historical record can deliver a true verdict on our deliberations.

Bibliography

Aeronautical Technologies for the Twenty-First Century, Committee on Aeronautical Technologies, Aeronautics and Space Engineering Board, Commission on Engineering and Technical Systems, National Research Council (National Academy Press, Washington, 1992).

Airbus.com/pdf/media/GMF2004_full_issue.pdf

Aluminum Now, (September/October, 2002).

Arnold and Porter, 'US Government Support of the US Commercial Aircraft Industry', (Washington DC, 1991).

Becher, T. *Boeing 757 and 767*, (Crowood, Marlborough, 1999).

Biddle, W, *Barons of the Sky*, (Henry Holt, New York, 1991).

Birtles, Philip, *Airlife's Airliners vol. 7: Boeing 767*, (Airlife, Shrewsbury, 1999).

'Boeing's Big Stall', *Washington Post*, (18 January, 1998).

Bowonder B. and Ramana Rao S. V. 'Creating and Sustaining Competitiveness – An Analysis of the World Civil Aircraft Industry', *World Competition, Law and Economics Review*, vol. 16, No.4, 1993, pp. 5-47.

Bright, C. D. *The Jet Makers*, (Regents of Kansas Press, Lawrence, 1978).

Business Week Online, (15 December, 2003).

*Business Week, (*13 April, 2005, June 20, 2005).

Cantor, D. 'Aircraft Production and the US Economy', in J.W. Fischer, (ed.), *Airbus Industrie: An Economic and Trade Perspective*, CRS Report to Congress, (Washington, 1992).

Chicago Tribune, (23 February, 2005).

Constant, E. W. *The Origins of the Turbojet Revolution,* (Johns Hopkins University Press, Baltimore, 1980).

The Daily Herald, (29 June, 2005).

Davies, R. E. G. *Supersonic (Airliner) Non-sense: A Case Study in Applied Market Research,* (Paladwr, McLean VA, 1998).

Dowdy, J. 'Winners and Losers in the Arms Industry Downturn', (*Foreign Policy,* Summer, 1997).

The Economist, (29 November, 2003).

The Financial Times, (23 September, 1997, 24 November, 2004).

Flight International, (26 August, 1998, 2 September, 1998, 9 December, 2003, 22-28 February, 2005).

Goldstein, J. 'Ideas, Institutions and American Trade Policy', in G. John Ikenberry, Lake, D. A. and Mastanduno, M. (eds), *The State and American Foreign Economic Policy*, (Cornell University Press, Ithaca, New York, 1988).

Golich, V 'From Competition to Cooperation: The Challenge of Commercial-class Aircraft Manufacturing', (*International Organization,* 46, 4, 1992).

'Government Support of the Large Commercial Aircraft Industries of Japan, Europe and the United States', report prepared for the Office of Technology Assessment of the Congress of the United States, (Washington, May, 1991).

The Guardian, (26 March, 1997).

Gunston, B. *Boeing Aircraft: The History of the Boeing Aircraft Company,* (Osprey, 1998, Oxford).

Guretsky, Lt Col. J. *The Boeing Company*, (Secretary of Defense, Fellows Program, Washington DC, 1999).

Hardy, M. J. *Boeing,* (Beaufort, New York, 1982).

Hayward, K. *The British Aircraft Industry,* (Manchester University Press, 1989).

——— 'Airbus: 20 Years of European Collaboration', *International Affairs*, vol. 64, No.1 (Winter 1987-88).

——— *International Collaboration in Civil Aerospace.* (Francis Pinter, London, 1986).

Heppenheimer, T. A. *Turbulent Skies,* (Wiley, New York, 1995).

Hochmuth, M. S. 'Aerospace' in *Big Business and the State*, Raymond Vernon (ed.), (Harvard University Press, Cambridge, Mass., 1974).

Hooks, G. *Forging the Military Industrial Complex,* (University of Illinois Press, Urbana, 1991).

Irving, C. *Widebody: the Triumph of the 747*, (William Morrow, New York, 1993).

Kent, R, *Safe, Separated and Soaring: a History of Federal Civil Aviation Policy 1961-1971*, (US Government Printing Office, Washington DC, 1980).

Klepper, G. 'Entry into the Market for Large Transport Aircraft' *European Economic Review,* vol. 34, No.4 (1990): 775-803, p. 780.

Komons, N. A. *Bonfires to Beacons: Federal Civil Aviation Policy under the Air Commerce Act, 1926-1938*, (Smithsonian Institution Press, Washington, 1989).

Krugman, P. R. and Obstfeld, M *International Economics*, (Harper Collins, New York, 1994).

www.leeham.net/default.asp?Page=27

www.leeham.net/filelib/ScottsColumn62805.pdf

Lawrence, P. K. and Dowdall, P. G. *Strategic Trade in Commercial Class Aircraft: EU versus USA*, (Royal Institute of International Affairs, 1998).

Lawrence, P. K. and Braddon, D. L. *Strategic Issues in European Aerospace,* (Ashgate, Aldershot, 1999).

Lawrence, P. K. *Aerospace Strategic Trade,* (Ashgate, Aldershot, 2001).

Lynn, M. *Birds of Prey, Boeing v. Airbus*, (Four Walls Eight Windows, New York, 1995).

MacPherson, A. and Pritchard, D., 'Outsourcing US Commercial Aircraft Technology and Innovation: Implications for the Industry's Long-Term Design and Build Capability', (Canada-United Sates Trade Centre Occasional paper, State University of Buffalo, New York, 2004).

Markusen, A. et al., *The Rise of the Gunbelt*, (Oxford University Press, Oxford, 1991, p. 56).

McIntyre, I. *Dog Fight: the Trans-Atlantic Battle over Airbus,* (Praeger, Westport, Conn. 1992).

Miller, R. and Sawers, D. *The Technical Development of Modern Aviation*, (Praeger, New York, 1970).

Mowery, D. and Rosenberg, N. 'The Commercial Aircraft Industry' in Nelson Richard R. (ed.), *Government and Technical Progress*, (Pergammon Press, New York, 1982).

Muller, P. *Airbus: L'Ambition Europeenne,* (L'Harmattan, Paris, 1989).

Newhouse, J. *The Sporty Game,* (Alfred Knopf, New York, 1982).

NASA FY1996 Appropriation Hearing (104th Congress, 1st Session, 1995).

NASA Office of Aeronautics, (FY1996 Budget report).

NASA, Langley Research Centre, *Spin-Off 97,* (NASA, 1997).

Noble, D. '*Command Performance: a Perspective on the Social and Economic Consequences of Military Enterprise*', in Smith M.R. (ed.), *Military Enterprise and Technological Change*, (MIT, Cambridge, Mass. 1987).

Norris, G. and Wagner, M. *Douglas Jetliners*, (MBI, Osceola WI, 1999).

Patillo, D. *Pushing the Envelope: The American Aircraft Industry*, (The University of Michigan Press, Ann Arbor, 2000).

Picq, J. *Les Ailes de l'Europe*, (Fayard, Paris, 1990).

Pinelli, T. et al., *Knowledge Diffusion in the US Aerospace Industry: the NASA/DoD Aerospace Knowledge Diffusion Project*, (Ablex Publishing, Westport, 1997).

Porter, M. E. (ed.), *Competition in Global Industries*. (Harvard Business School Press, Cambridge, 1986).

Rodgers, E. *Flying High: the Story of Boeing and the Rise of the Jetliner Industry*, (The Atlantic Monthly Press, New York, 1996).

Sabbagh, K. *Twenty-First Century Jet*, (Scribner, New York, 1996).

Sampson, A. *The Arms Bazaar*, (Viking Press, New York, 1977).

———— *Empires of the Sky: The Politics, Contests and Cartels of World Airlines,* (Hodder and Stoughton, London, 1984).

Seattle Post Intelligencer, (5 January 2005).

Seattle Weekly, (3-9 December 2003, 1-7 December 2004).

Sherry, M. A. *The Rise of American Airpower: the Creation of Armageddon,* (Yale University Press, New Haven, 1988).

Solberg, C. *Conquest of the Skies: a History of Commercial Aviation in America,* (Little, Brown and Co. New York, 1979).

www.speednews.com/lists/1Q05O&D.pdf

Sunday Business, (11 February, 2001).

Taneja, N. K. *The International Airline Industry*, (Lexington Books, Lanham, 1988).

Thornton, D. W. *Airbus Industrie: The Politics of an International Industrial Collaboration*, (Macmillan, London, 1995).

Tucker, J. 'Partners and Rivals: a Model of International Collaboration in Advanced Technology', (*International Organisation*, 45, Winter, 2001).

Tyson, L. D. *Who's Bashing Whom? Trade Conflict in High Technology Industries,* (International Institute for International Economics, Washington DC, 1992).

Vander Meulen, J. A. *The Politics of Aircraft: Building an American Military Industry*, (University Press of Kansas, Lawrence, 1992).

Van Scherpenberg, J. 'International Competition and European Defence Industries', (*International Affairs*, vol. 75, No. 3, 1997).

Wall Street Journal, (30 July, 1991).

Wall Street Journal, (21 February, 2005).

Washington Post, (18 January, 1998).

Wilson, J. R. *Turbulence Aloft: The Civil Aeronautics Administration Amid Wars and Rumors of Wars, 1938-1953*, (Department of Transportation, Federal Aviation Administration, Washington, 1979).

http://en.wikipedia.org/wiki/General_Electric_GENX

Yoshino, M. Y. 'Global Competition in a Salient Industry: The Case of Civil Aircraft' in Porter, M. E. (ed), *The Competition in Global Industries,* (Harvard Business School Press, Boston, 1986).

Index